TRAVELER'S GUIDE TO BATUU

BLACK SPIRE OUTPOST AND BEYOND

by Eloc Throno

CONTENTS

DOCKING BAY 9

THE SPACEPORT

THE MARKET

THE FOREST

QUICK REFERENCE GUIDE

WELCOME TO BATUU

Like so many travelers who came before, I love Batuu. This once-bustling crossroads has evolved over the generations. Today, it is a popular destination for traders, smugglers, artisans, and adventurers alike. Off the beaten path, Batuu is exotic and charming, remote yet full of life, peaceful but at times perilous. For travelers willing to venture outside of the well-trodden hyperspace routes and try something a little different, Batuu will reward you with a rich experience thanks to its unique blend of cultures and opportunities.

I hope when you arrive you will be overcome with the desire to explore all this wonderful place has to offer. I also hope that this guide might help you get the most out of your journey. Take a moment to marvel at the ships coming and going from the spaceport. Explore the natural beauty of the Surabat River Valley. Have a drink at an eclectic cantina while listening to the myriad languages spoken around you. Look up at the black spire and consider all of the beings who have come before.

I've spent more than two decades exploring the galaxy and can say with certainty that Batuu's allure is unmatched. For that reason, I return to Batuu time and again to update this guide, talk to the people, and experience the planet as the locals do. I hope to see you there soon.

Now and 'til the Spire!
Eloc Throno
Galaxy Adventurer

EXPLORE BATUU

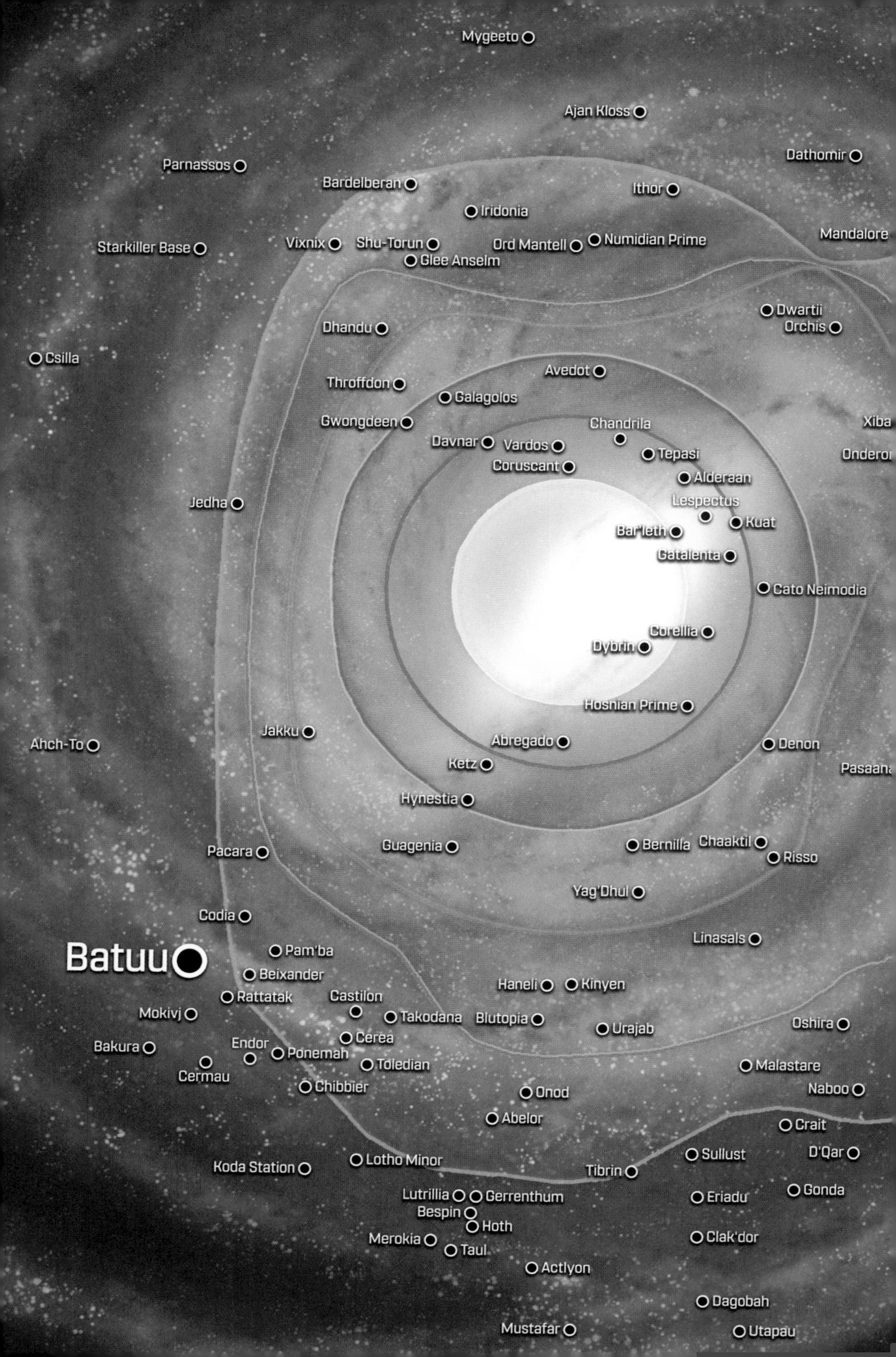

Mygeeto

Ajan Kloss

Dathomir

Parnassos

Bardelberan

Ithor

Mandalore

Iridonia

Numidian Prime

Starkiller Base

Vixnix   Shu-Torun
          Glee Anselm

Ord Mantell

Dwartii
Orchis

Dhandu

Csilla

Avedot

Throffdon

Galagolos

Chandrila

Xiba

Gwongdeen

Davnar   Vardos

Tepasi

Onderon

Coruscant

Alderaan

Lespectus

Jedha

Bar'leth

Kuat

Gatalenta

Cato Neimodia

Corellia

Dybrin

Hoshian Prime

Jakku

Ahch-To

Abregado

Denon

Ketz

Pasaana

Hynestia

Pacara

Guagenia

Bernilla   Chaaktil

Risso

Yag'Dhul

Codia

Linasals

Batuu

Pam'ba

Beixander

Haneli   Kinyen

Rattatak

Castilon

Mokivj

Takodana   Blutopia

Oshira

Cerea

Urajab

Bakura

Endor   Ponemah

Malastare

Cermau

Toledian

Naboo

Chibbier

Onod

Crait

Abelor

Sullust

D'Qar

Koda Station

Lotho Minor

Tibrin

Eriadu

Gonda

Lutrillia   Gerrenthum
Bespin

Merokia   Hoth

Clak'dor

Taul

Actlyon

Dagobah

Mustafar

Utapau

GALAXY MAP

As you see, Batuu is in the Western Reaches of the Outer Rim, perched on the edge of the known and unknown. It is precisely this location that has shaped the planet's history. Before advanced hyperspace capabilities, Batuu's position made it a bustling fueling stop for ships heading into Wild Space. With the advances technology and well-charted hyperlanes, most modern travelers choose to bypass Batuu, resulting in the planet becoming a crossroads for adventurers and a haven for those who prefer life in the shadows.

MAP KEY

- Planets of the galaxy
- Deep Core
- Core
- Colonies
- Inner Rim
- Expansion Region
- Mid Rim
- Outer Rim
- Hutt Space

enno
Moraband
Cantonica
Florrum
Cholganna
Karkaris
Yavin
Felucia
Mon Cala
Atollon
Chad
Lothal
Garel
Mooga
Kijimi
Saleucami
Sriluur
Vodran
Kintan
Kashyyyk
Oba Diah
Kessel
Toydaria
Nal Hutta
Teth
yacan
Ketzali
Vandor
Gamorr
Eroudac
Rishi
Scarif
Ando
Kowak
Zolan
Rodia
Tatooine
Wick
Christophsis
Geonosis
Savareen
Ryloth
Pantora

GETTING TO BATUU

Although Batuu lies on the far edge of the Outer Rim, off-worlders have many options for travel to the planet.

Batuu does not lie on a major hyperspace lane, but finding it is relatively easy with most standard navicomputers or a seasoned pilot. Use proper caution on final approach to Batuu: Disorderly smugglers have been known to engage in starship skirmishes in the space around the planet. Unsuspecting pilots can get caught in the crossfire of these dangerous clashes.

Galactic Coordinates. -401.72, -561.84, 004.32

BY PERSONAL OR HIRED STARSHIP

The Black Spire Outpost Spaceport offers short-term starship docking on a first-come, first served basis. Payments for these docking bays can be made to Oga Garra, who also runs the outpost's popular cantina (and most of the town). Long-term leases are available but failing to pay on time is ill-advised. I don't recommend testing Oga's patience. Those wishing to avoid docking fees will find **landing fields** just outside of town. The walk to the Outpost is long, however, and I advise only parking on the outskirts if you have your own speeder. You'll not only be better rested upon your arrival, but you'll have more time to explore the town itself.

A NOTE ON WILD SPACE

Batuu lies on the edge of **Wild Space** of the galaxy. As the name implies, this remote area is largely unexplored and holds many secrets. Only the most adventurous travelers should even consider a trip through these regions. Few guides, maps, and resources are available to travelers who wish to venture into this region. If you're crazy enough to venture farther than Batuu, you don't need a guide!

BY STARCRUISER

The **Chandrila Star Line** are now offering voyages aboard their legendary starcruiser the *Halcyon*. Travelers who appreciate glamour and adventure can lodge in their well-appointed cabins and take advantage of unique excursions to Batuu during the day. For those who appreciate travel at its finest, the service and experience are unrivaled anywhere in the galaxy. This Corellian MPO-1400 starcruiser brings an unmatched level of elegance and sophistication to this wild corner of the galaxy.

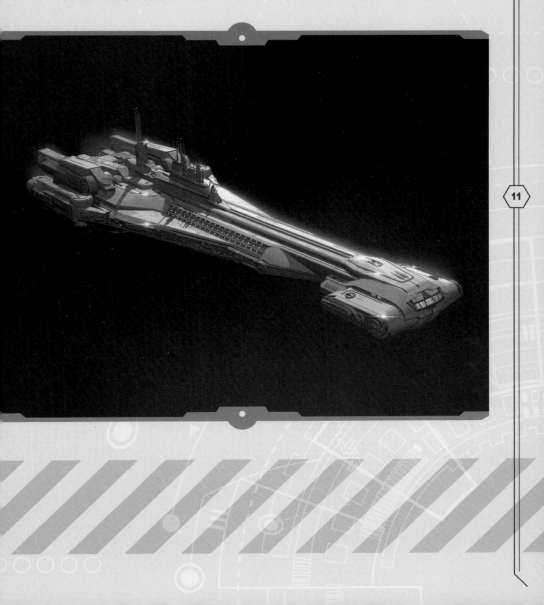

NEED TO KNOW: FAST FACTS TO HELP YOU ON YOUR JOURNEY

Climate. Batuu offers a temperate climate that is enjoyable by most species. Its **oxygen atmosphere** is breathable by most, though some species should plan to pack their own respirators if not accustomed to oxygen. Mon Cala, Quarren, Rodians, and other species from aquatic planets will find the air dry, but tolerable, even for an extended stay. The occasional afternoon rain shower is possible.

Dress. Don't be the traveler who overpacks their cargo for a trip to Batuu. I recommend light clothing worn in layers so that you are prepared for any occasion. If you forget to pack an item, you'll find alternatives for sale in Black Spire Outpost.

Language. With its diverse population, you might hear a variety of languages on Batuu. Huttese, Twi'leki, and Ithorian are common, but **Galactic Basic** is the primary language. Even those species who can't speak Basic will likely understand common phrases. I recommend you leave your translator droid at home and try your hand at a new language. It's a fun way to immerse yourself in the local culture and connect with a stranger. When in doubt, use the translator on your datapad.

Documentation. Some locals and especially the newly arrived First Order might ask to see your identification. Use your own judgement if this is wise and be wary of beings who might be looking to steal your identification card. Those arriving by starship and docking at the local spaceports will find helpful **docking permits** and registration forms provided in the back of this guide.

Currency. Galactic credits and the local money, **Batuuan Spira**, are the most common currencies used on the planet. With either credits or Spira, you will be able to purchase nearly all the meals, sundries, transportation, and lodging you need for a short-term journey. Most merchants have modern credit transactor terminals that will accept credit chips. Other currencies might be accepted at the merchant's discretion.

Crime. Travelers to Batuu typically don't find trouble unless they are looking for it. Though crime against tourists is rare, travelers should keep their guards up. **Smuggler's Alley** in Black Spire Outpost is perhaps the most notorious part of town, as the local boss, Oga Garra, now reserves its use exclusively for her smuggling crews. The local police force has long been disbanded, so travelers will have to fend for themselves.

Refreshers. Travelers who need to use the facilities will find refreshers ('freshers, for short) in various locations on Black Spire Outpost and a few other settlements on Batuu, but those traveling to the more remote areas of the planet are not so lucky. Look at the experience as a way to get more familiar with the natural surroundings or just try not to think of it at all.

Technology. Bringing your own handheld **comlink** or larger **datapad** is highly recommended. Make sure they are well charged as they will help you navigate the planet and tap into the local data feeds. The local radio feed, station **BSO 401.72**, offers news and entertainment programming in and around Black Spire Outpost.

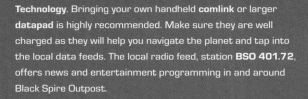

BATUU COMMUNITIES

For many, the planet Batuu is synonymous with its infamous settlement, Black Spire Outpost. While that is the most populated landmark, Batuu offers even more to explore during longer excursions.

Black Spire Outpost is the largest settlement on Batuu and my recommendation for new and returning visitors alike. Named for the ancient petrified trees that tower above the outpost, it has quietly become a vital stop for traders, adventurers, smugglers, and others. Here you will find spaceports, a colorful marketplace, a variety of food options, and most of the vital services. You could spend days getting lost in its streets and exploring its history. From Black Spire (as the locals call it), you'll have access to the beautiful plains, majestic mountains, and flowing rivers of Batuu.

The **Galma District** is a short shuttle ride from Black Spire Outpost. To many it feels undeveloped, as most of the structures here have been scavenged and repurposed. Broken-down speeders and ships serve as homes and workshops for the resourceful mechanics who live here today. It has a rich tradition of high-speed podracing, illegal since the days of the Old Republic. These activities attract a criminal element and I do not recommend it for most off-worlders. Gambling on these activities is a quick way to lose all your credits and you do not want to be in debt to anyone who frequents this district. The Galma symbol represents a disconnected circle to signify the scoundrel attitude of always finding a way.

Another residential community not far from Black Spire Outpost, the **Surabat** vicinity is located in the beautiful Surabat River Valley. The hardy residents, though isolated, build sturdy homes that sit nestled against the base of the beautiful spires and mountains. Weather here is more harsh than other parts of Batuu, with strong winds throughout the year. The town is tiny and offers few modern conveniences, but it remains a favorite jumping-off point for mountain hikers and thrill-seekers looking to climb the ancient spires. Many who live here sustain themselves as lichen harvesters, bravely climbing the spires to collect valuable **golden lichen** (for more on lichen, see page 20). Local legend says that this is the site where a group of children disappeared many decades ago, but the generally reserved residents rarely speak of this event to outsiders. The Surabat symbol represents the iconic Surabat River Valley to signify the heart and hardiness of the community.

What the **Peka Community** lacks in size it makes up for in majestic beauty. I find the residents here welcoming and sociable to visitors, willing to share their modest, family-oriented lives with those who pass through. The people of Peka are naturalists who survive off the land around them. Many work as fishermen and farmers, some even offering to take off-worlders on fishing excursions that let you catch and cook your own lunch on the banks of the flowing river. This river community is noted for its simple tents, huts, and log cabins built from the native trees, but lodging for guests is limited. The Peka symbol represents a drop of water in the Peka river to signify the ripple effects their choices can make on the community.

Agricultural communities dot every corner of Batuu. Though they often provide the food you'll enjoy at Black Spire Outpost, few travelers make their way to these remote communities. Even if your journey will not take you to one of these villages, know that you will support the local economy by purchasing many of the dishes offered at the local eateries.

A HISTORY OF BATUU

ANCIENT TIMES

Batuu was once home to an ancient civilization. While little is known about the people and culture of this lost society, their legacy can still be seen today. Batuu is dotted with ruins from this eons-old civilization. While rumors persist that the caves remain booby-trapped by the ancient settlers, and some intrepid smugglers have been known to use the ruins to hide illicit goods, their passageways and caverns are perfect for modern explorers who enjoy history or architecture.

FIRST SETTLERS

Long after Batuu's ancient culture disappeared, settlers turned the planet into a crossroads for trade. They founded Black Spire Outpost, naming it for the one iconic petrified black tree trunk that stands prominently in the heart of the Outpost (next to Dok-Ondar's Den of Antiquities). This particular trunk is blacker in color than the rest of the spires, which dot the planet landscape after millions of years. Before the modern hyperspace lanes were established, Batuu was an important stop for traders traveling through this sector of the galaxy. Its market grew over time, bringing culture and modest wealth to the planet. Though it has lost some of that importance today, it remains an attractive stopover for those who wish to stay off of the beaten path. Today, the most obvious reminder of this era of Batuu's history can be found at Black Spire Outpost's market. The bazaar there retains the architecture and atmosphere of old Batuu, alive with trade and travelers. Walking down its cobbled streets is like stepping into the past.

RECENT PAST

During the High Republic, the Jedi established a small research station in the wilds of the planet. Today, Batuu is a bustling crossroads that mostly attracts people who don't want to be noticed. Senator Padmé Amidala, who represented Naboo in the Galactic Senate during the Clone Wars, was spotted briefly near Black Spire. Years later, locals spoke about the visit by the legendary Darth Vader during the time of the Galactic Empire.

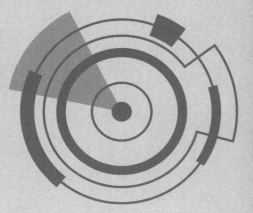

CURRENT AFFAIRS:
POLITICS & BATUU

It's been about thirty years since the end of the Galactic Civil War and the fall of the Galactic Empire. The **New Republic** rose to take its place and was the largest ruling power in the galaxy for some thirty years. That was until recently.

 Much of the galaxy is still in shock after the destruction of the Hosnian System. The planet served as the seat of government for the New Republic, its Galactic Senate, and its starfleet. Millions reported seeing a red beam of energy streak through space just before reports surfaced about Hosnian Prime's destruction, but experts and average citizens alike still debate what they saw. Some believe that it was the **First Order** that destroyed the New Republic, but others have their doubts. Clearly, the First Order wields a strong military, but the ability to destroy an entire system from across the galaxy is a feat that even the old Death Star battle stations could not accomplish.

In any case, the First Order is seizing the opportunity to make themselves known to the wider galaxy. In these parts, scattered reports of the First Order have existed for years, but now the sound of stormtroopers on the march rings out unmistakably in star systems far and wide. With the New Republic leadership gone, there is little to stop their advance through the galaxy.

Depending on how you look at them, the **Resistance** led by former Rebel Alliance General Leia Organa, is made up of either freedom fighters or instigators. Their supporters insist that this small band is all that remains to stand up against the tyranny of the First Order. Others suggest that they are war-mongers: rebels who were unwilling to let go of the old fight. It is indisputable that the Resistance lacks the material might of the First Order, but nonetheless fills its ranks with those willing to rally behind their cause.

Batuu has no formal government of its own and has never played a major role in galactic politics. Yet on my most recent visit, it has become clear that not even this remote outpost is immune from outside pressures. The First Order has landed at Black Spire Outpost and they've made their presence known. Outside the outpost, there is even evidence of Resistance forces gathering nearby. No matter what your political allegiances, visitors should be alert during this time of heightened tension.

FLORA AND FAUNA OF BATUU

Batuu is a planet of many natural wonders, the most obvious of which are its **petrified trees**. Eons ago, these massive trees rose to unimaginable heights. Just the trunks remain today, but even now they are the most prominent feature of the planet's landscape. Gone are the gargantuan trees of old and now a smaller species—known as **Batuu trees**—fill in much of the planet surface. The dark green conifers have robust roots that grow into stony soil and cling to rocky surfaces. They serve as home to the common **terra tree toads**.

GOLDEN LICHEN

The ancient petrified tree trunks are the home of another distinct type of flora: **golden lichen**. Known as "gold dust" to the locals, the lichen grows throughout Black Spire Outpost and the Surabat River Valley. The lichen serves many purposes on Batuu, including as a clothing dye and a garnish ingredient for cooking. While the residents of the Surabat vicinity are best known for harvesting the valuable resource, its Oga Garra who gets the most out of this special substance. She has a virtual monopoly on its cultivation and exportation. Travelers should not attempt to harvest any lichen themselves, as Oga's wrath is more dangerous than the perilous climb to reach it!

Travelers should beware of the local rumor that invisible, **poisonous anemone** live in the water pools of the ancient ruins. I'm not one to test my luck and always caution other travelers against entering or drinking from untreated water.

You might encounter a variety of common species during your stay here. Listen for the songs of the **pipa birds**, rarely seen but often heard among the forests after sunrise. At night, watch for the lights of **spiran fireflies** that descend from the spires and put on a multicolor lightshow. **Batuuan rats** are famously brazen and can survive in the wilderness or urban areas alike. The rats serve as an important food source for the **nightsnake**, which can be encountered among the forests just outside Black Spire Outpost.

With so many visitors passing through Batuu over the centuries, with them came species from other planets. These days, it's hard to tell what is truly native to Batuu and what arrived thanks to interplanetary travel. One such foreign species is the **can-cell**. I've seen them in my travels to Kashyyyk, Rodia, Taul, Teth, Ryloth, and now widespread throughout Batuu. Spot them by their four distinctive quad wings and largely insect eyes while flying at higher altitudes.

CAN-CELL

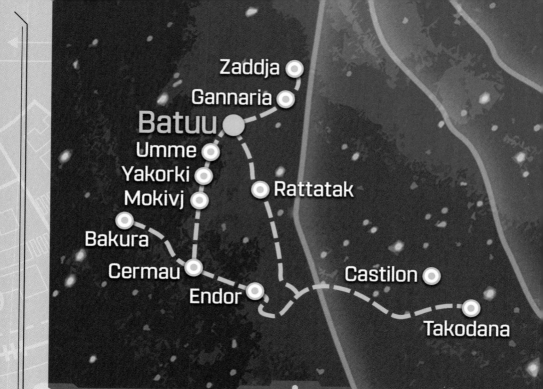

DAY TRIPS FROM BATUU

Batuu is the perfect home base to reach a variety of interesting destinations.
These are all popular locales that are just a short flight away.

 Travelers looking for a big city within a reasonable commute should
consider **Bakura**. Its capital city of Salis D'aar is conveniently laid
out in a circular pattern, making it easy for outsiders to navigate.
The city dwarfs Black Spire Outpost and offers all of the modern
conveniences, though the planet itself pales in comparison to Batuu's
natural beauty.

 The **Forest Moon of Endor** is a perfect day trip for those interested
in both nature and history. Its towering trees are home to tribes of
Ewoks, generally now friendly to off-worlders. Military history buffs
will appreciate the moon's role in the Galactic Civil War. If piloting
your own starship, be aware of the debris field in orbit above the moon,
a relic of the famous battle where the Rebel Alliance destroyed the
second Death Star.

Another planet in the Trilon sector, **Gannaria** sees far fewer visitors than Batuu. Those who do are most likely engaging in the illegal spice trade that has existed on the planet for hundreds of years. Black Spire Outpost is a convenient stop for smugglers who take illegal trips to and from the planet.

 Travel to **Mokivj**, once known for its beautiful sunsets and ten moons, is no longer a recommended destination. The catastrophic lava flows devastated the planet's ecosystem decades ago and it has never fully recovered from the tragic event.

 Simple yet beautiful architecture awaits you on **Rattatak**, a mountainous planet with humble communities seemingly carved out of the surrounding sandstone rock. Please note that historically it has been a place notorious for its warlords and gladiatorial societies. Proceed with caution, should you choose an excursion to this planet.

 Once one of my most high-recommended day trips from Batuu, **Takodana** has lost some it's appeal recently. While I used to recommend Maz Kanata's castle for food and lodging, its recent destruction makes me hesitant to suggest this lush planet of forests and lakes for your itinerary.

 Nearby **Umme** offers galaxy-class hunting. Bring your own big-game blaster or use one provided by one of the many guide services. Most of those who can afford to travel to this remote planet can afford full-service safari guides who take care of mobile accommodations, droid porters, game tracking, and field taxidermy.

 Yakork is best known for its wide selection of edible fungi. The annual Fungi Fest is a must-see pilgrimage for many, attracting thousands of visitors each cycle. The planet has limited exports, so travelers must venture here to experience all the delicacies it has to offer.

Archipelagoes of white sand beaches welcome you to **Zaddja**, where locals live on flying skiffs. At night, the high tides cover the shallow beaches with sea water and the land disappears entirely.

EXPLORE BLACK SPIRE OUTPOST

MUST SEE: BLACK SPIRE OUTPOST

For first-timers or returning travelers alike, these are my must-see sights at Black Spire Outpost.

1 **Cantina**. Oga Garra's Cantina is the hub of activity at Black Spire. Whether you need a drink or a job, you'll find both here surrounded by some of the Outpost's most interesting inhabitants.

2 **Spaceport**. Even if you don't fly to Black Spire Outpost, I recommend a stop at the spaceport to truly appreciate the Outpost's bustling trade. Watch ships of all types come and go, filled with interesting crews and exotic cargoes.

3 **The Market**. Walking through the market is a feast for the senses. Shoppers here find an unparalleled array of goods from Batuu and beyond.

Old Outpost. Reminders of Batuu's ancient past lie just outside the city walls. Explore the cavernous ruins while you search for clues about a mysterious civilization long gone.

4

Dok-Ondar's Den of Antiquities. Renowned collector and merchant Dok-Ondar has spent a century in Black Spire Outpost gathering curiosities and antiques from every corner of the galaxy. You can get lost in his shop where every item has a unique story to tell.

5

Docking Bay 7 Food and Cargo. A rotating selection of chefs come from far and wide to sell culinary delights at this docking bay. A quick meal here will not soon be forgotten.

6

Milk Stand. Weary travelers and hard-working locals alike will find the refreshments at Bubo Wamba's Milk Stand the perfect pick-me-up on any day. You can't go wrong with both the locally farmed bantha milk and the imported green milk.

7

THE FORCE

The Gatherers of Black Spire Outpost believe in the Force, a mystical energy that comes from all living things. They are just one of the many sects across the galaxy who teach of this ancient power. While not all that follow the ways of the Force have the ability to tap into its power, some of the more exceptional being can harness the Force through unique abilities. Telekinesis, persuasion, and visions are all known Force abilities.

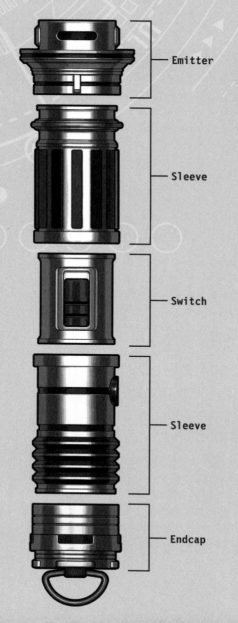

Emitter

Sleeve

Switch

Sleeve

Endcap

One item most commonly associated with Force users is the ancient energy blade weapon, the lightsaber. The elegant weapon is exceedingly rare, as most of them (and their users) were destroyed by the Galactic Empire half a century ago. Lightsabers of old were made from almost every imaginable material, representing the wielders who made them.

At the heart of the lightsaber is a kyber crystal. The rare crystal occurs naturally in the environment, including most famously on the moon of Jedha. The crystal focuses the energy of the blade and gives the laser sword its unique color.

Kyber Crystal

THE PEOPLE OF BLACK SPIRE

The allure of Black Spire has long brought travelers of all types to the old galactic crossroads. This old settler's song says more about the people of Batuu than any other.

AT THE EDGE OF THE GALAXY,
SO FAR AWAY
BLACK WAS THE SPIRE
THAT CALLED ME TO STAY

A BEACON FOR DRIFTERS
FORGOTTEN AND LOST
THE SPIRES SUMMONED
THOSE BROKEN AND TOSSED

COME STAY HERE FOREVER,
OR JUST PASS ON THROUGH
THE SPIRIT OF BLACK SPIRE
WILL FOREVER CHANGE YOU

LAND PORT

THE LAND PORT

Many who arrive at Black Spire will enter through the unkept roads of the **Land Port**. It serves as the entry way for travelers on foot, creatures, and speeders alike. More industrial than other parts of the Outpost, it lacks some of the charm you might find farther in town but is no less important of a stop on your journey. Here on the outskirts you will find an array of important services and shops. Notable businesses nearby include **Black Spire Station**, offering fuel and repairs for speeders; the **Droid Depot**; and the local scrapping operation's main office otherwise known as **Savi's Workshop**.

LANDSPEEDERS

Locals employ a wide variety of ground transportation to travel between Black Spire Outpost and outlying villages. While they might not be the latest technology or most luxurious models found today, the industrial inhabitants of Batuu keep their speeders running season after season. Rugged, reliable craft such as these are among the many you might find during your visit.

Model: X-34 Landspeeder
Length: 3.4 meters
Maximum Speed: 250 kilometers/hour
Maximum Altitude: 1 meter

Model: V-35 Courier
Manufacturer: SoroSuub Corporation
Length: 3.8 meters
Maximum Speed: 120 kilometers/hour
Passengers: 1 crew, 3 passengers

Model: Aratech 74-Z
Manufacturer: Aratech Repulsor Company
Length: 3.2 meters
Maximum Speed: 360 kilometers/hour
Passengers: 1 crew, 1 passenger

Model: Undicur Jumpspeeder
Manufacturer: Kuat Vehicles
Length: 1.84 meters
Maximum Speed: 250 kilometers/hour

BLACK SPIRE STATION

This outpost does not have a dedicated refueling station for landspeeders but fuel and repairs are available at **Black Spire Station**. It's part junkyard, part garage, and almost always open for business. Don't let the mess fool you: this is your best option for quality mechanical work. Speeder parking is available nearby and the rest of Black Spire is just a convenient walk away.

SALJU

When I return to Batuu, I always look forward to seeing **Salju** at Black Spire Station. Born and raised nearby, she loves to hear my stories about life outside of this planet. Her enthusiasm is infectious and she is always happy to meet new travelers. Anyone who stumbles into her station will surely face cheerful questions from the inquisitive native. That curiosity fuels her work as a tinkerer and I consider her the best mechanic on Black Spire. She loves to pass along her expertise to travelers and takes a particular liking to young strays who pass through, such as the local loth-cat pictured below. If you are looking for speeder parts, there's a good chance you'll find them among her collection (or hoard, depending on how you look at it).

Traveling to Batuu after winter, I was once witness to a wonderful scene in the Surabat River Valley. That day, like every year, Salju met up with her old friend **Elee**. The two were raised together as sisters until Elee grew too large for Salju's family home. Now Elee lives with a family of her own species in Surabat River Valley, but reunites with Salju after her winter hibernation to frolic and play just as they were children.

ⅅⅮⅭⅮ ⅮⅭⅮⅭⅮ

DROID DEPOT

Across the street from Black Spire Station lies the **Droid Depot**. The collection of droids outside and the distinctive logo on the wall make this shop hard to miss. Alternatively, simply follow the beeps and chirps to this haven for mechanical beings. Stepping inside to the front office you'll find Black Spire's most complete collection of droids, technical manuals, droid parts, and tools. Tucked outside the shop lies a repair station and oil bath, normally considered a luxury by most droid companions. No one knows when the oil was last changed, however, so bathe at your own risk.

If you are looking for a new droid, R-series and BB-series astromechs are well stocked and offered for sale at fair market rates. Buying a droid directly from the depot allows you to customize your new mech in the **Droid Build Room**, a well-appointed workshop offering a selection of droid bodies, heads, conveniently prepainted panels, and those all-important motivators.

MUBO

For droid sales and repairs, look no further than Mubo. This delightfully quirky Utai is a technical wizard and a sixth-generation droid builder on Batuu. Many of the droids you see around town passed through Mubo's shop, including the DJ droid at the cantina and the pitmaster at Ronto Roasters. Though Mubo can be a little eccentric and is easily distracted, his droid creations are as unique as he is. Mubo tends to stick to himself, but is never too shy to help a fellow droid builder. His work has been piling up as of late, so don't take offense if he can't tend to your droid immediately. Luckily, helpful **droid repair technicians** are always on hand to help you select, build, or modify your next droid. Their passion and knowledge about droids always impress me. I find their selection of astromechs to be particularly robust whether you want a classic R-series model or the latest advancements in droid technology.

DROID BUYER'S GUIDE

Droids are a helpful—and sometimes necessary—companion during your galactic travels. The ability to perform repairs or translate alien languages is always helpful, but don't underestimate their value as friends. The bond you form with a droid can last for a lifetime. This handy buyer's guide will help you decide which model is right for you

ASTROMECH DROIDS

BB-series. Discerning buyers seeking the latest technology will love the BB-series astromechs. Their spherical bodies offer superior mobility to the older R-series and tool bay discs deliver maximum flexibility.

R-series. Industrial Automaton's R-series astromech has been the galaxy's best seller for decades. Offered in a variety of configurations, you're sure to find one to suit your needs. Pilots, mechanics, and farmers alike swear by these trusty and dependable droids.

C1-series. Outdated and sometimes erratic, I prefer other models.

RATING KEY:

WOULD NOT
RECOMMEND

EXCELLENT

POWER DROIDS

EG-6 series. Commonly referred to as "gonk" droids, these walking batteries mostly escape notice as they go about their mundane tasks. If you need portable power for starships or machinery, this is your best bet.

REPAIR DROIDS

WED Treadwell. Many swear by the utility offered by the Treadwell droid. They have a tool arm for nearly every job and can be acquired for a reasonable price on the secondary market.

MSE-series. Don't let their small size fool you, the "mouse" droid excels at cleaning, routine maintenance tasks, and running diagnostics.

3PO. Protocol droids serve as personal aides by specializing in translation and etiquette. Government officials and dignitaries rarely travel without one.

RA-7. Once commonly found in Imperial service, the Arakyd Industries droid can be found at surplus prices today.

MAINTENANCE GUIDE

Proper maintenance of your droid is essential. I recommend you perform these tasks at regular intervals.

1 Always fit unfamiliar droids with a restraining bolt to ensure they follow commands.

2 I recommend monthly oil baths, and even more frequently in sandy climates. An oil bath helps lubricate gears and protects your droid's finish. Only use well maintained baths with clean, high-performance droid oil.

BATTLE DROIDS

B1 battle droid. These relics of the Clone Wars weren't effective in their time and aren't recommended today.

⬡⬡⬡⬡⬡

SECURITY DROIDS

KX-series security droid. These capable droids are hard to find since the fall of the Empire. Well-maintained examples fetch steep prices thanks to the variety of tasks they can perform, including security and intelligence gathering.

⬡⬡⬡⬡⬡

3 Visually inspect all tool attachments and appendages for wear and tear. Replace as needed.

4 If your droid becomes temperamental, performing a memory wipe will return them to peak efficiency.

SAVI'S WORKSHOP

Though many pass by this ordinary building in the Land Port, on a recent trip to Black Spire I overheard some travelers suggest that there is more to this shop than meets the eye. **Savi's Workshop** certainly looks unassuming from the outside. Officially, it is the front office for the **Savi and Son Salvage** company that runs the salvage yard across town. Taking a peek inside, you'll see that the office is a packrat's paradise, filled with the very best salvaged parts to pass through the junkyard.

The most special items found here are curated by the "**Gatherers**." They clearly take their jobs here very seriously, but always strike me as casual and fun when I see them about. You might say that they are some of the most spiritual people here in the Outpost too. While I've never seen any of them use the **Force** themselves, they speak with great passion about restoring balance to the galaxy and seem eager to pass on their knowledge of the ancient religion.

Though I've spoken many times to the Gatherers about the Force, on my last visit I saw something I never expected. Standing inside the shop I heard a traveler tell the Gatherers, "I'm here to gather some parts. Savi sent me." With this seemingly ordinary request, the traveler was whisked away. A bit later, this traveler emerged wearing what looked to be a lightsaber on her belt!

Rarely visited by anyone, Jakku is a haven for scavengers thanks to the historic battle that took place there. This planet served as the final confrontation between the New Republic and Imperial forces. Scavengers salvage the ruined ships and armor for useful parts. Want to visit this desert planet yourself? Transport to Jakku can sometimes be arranged at the spaceport from private starship captains.

TRILON WISHING TREE

In the courtyard of Savi's Workshop stands a local landmark, the **Trilon Wishing Tree**. It's named for Batuu's home sector, Trilon. Hanging on the tree's branches are colorful strips of fabric. The multicolor bouquet is not only beautiful to behold, it represents the hopes and dreams of the locals. Each piece represents a wish or promise made to another. Local legend says that when the fabric or rope wears off, the wish is granted by the universe. Out of respect for those who left wishes here, please do not disrupt any of the pieces hanging from the tree.

43

MERCHANT ROW

Down this busy street lie some of Batuu's most famous (or infamous) businesses.
Built more recently than other parts of town, Merchant Row is home to the planet's
finest cantina and its most notorious shop. Walking here, you get the sense that all
of Batuu's most famous visitors and powerful players strolled this busy street too.

Give yourself plenty of time to explore Merchant Row.
I've known many travelers who lose track of time while
marveling at the items for sale here or taking in a
drink at Oga's Cantina. Just watch your step: this part
of town can be a little rough.

THE MUST-SEE ATTRACTIONS AT MERCHANT ROW

The liveliest spot around is **Oga's Cantina**. Its colorful patrons put on a symphony for the senses each day as they down a few drinks with friends, business partners, and the occasional rival.

Galaxy-renowned collector **Dok-Ondar** chose this part of town for his **Den of Antiquities**. It's a collector's paradise and regarded as the finest such shop of its kind in this corner of the galaxy. A stop at Dok's is a must-do for collectors and the curious alike.

In an underappreciated corner of Merchant Row lies Bubo Wamba's **Milk Stand**. Fresh milk in the green and blue varieties flow from this small but popular stop.

OGA'S CANTINA

Step up to the cantina at Black Spire Outpost and you'll be met with the aromas of exotic drinks and the sound of animated patrons' lively chatter (or is it fighting?) inside. If you're looking for action and intrigue in the Outpost, you've come to the right place. Here you're just as likely to find a job as you are a good drink. The cantina is where business gets done on Batuu. Owned by a Blutopian named **Oga Garra**, she takes great pride in her establishment and is always looking for new ways to bring in customers. She knows that as long as the cantina is the center of activity at Black Spire Outpost, she can call the shots.

In her eighty-two years in this galaxy, Oga has managed to rise from an orphan raised by the Hutts to become the boss of the entire outpost. In the last decade, she's become the most powerful figure in town. From docking permits to farm imports, she gets a cut of everything. Business doesn't get done on Black Spire Outpost without Oga's blessing and her approval isn't free. Anyone who tries to undermine her will soon discover her legendary temper. As a traveler, you shouldn't have any problems, as long as you don't stick your nose where it doesn't belong (whether you have a nose or not!).

OGA GARRA

Despite her great influence here, Oga rarely comes out of her office in the cantina. She has eyes and ears everywhere, reporting back on the goings-on across the outpost. If something is amiss or someone is trying to cut her out of some profits, you can bet she'll hear about it. And you can bet she won't tolerate it for long. A mere mention of her name makes the locals nervous, as her reputation has grown to almost mythical proportions. Even though most have never even seen her, they tell tall tales of her exploits. In recent days, word of the First Order's arrival has some speculating that she will make a rare appearance to stand up to their presence. Others say she will just lie low and patiently wait them out.

The cantina was remodeled about twenty years ago (that's recent by Outpost standards). Yet for its new exterior and interior, hints of the past still linger. Take the **blaster marks** on the wall, for example. Locals say those ended up there before Oga took over, scorched into the permacrete when a blue-skinned Imperial officer named **Grand Admiral Thrawn** got into a blaster fight with a group of off-worlders known as the Darshi. These little reminders are proof that the cantina was a rough place long before Oga got here.

DRINKS AT OGA'S CANTINA

Oga's Cantina is best known for its drink selection, a reputation that is well earned. The centerpiece of the cantina is the stone bar that wraps around the center of the room. On each side you'll find twenty-one drink dispensers—that's forty-two taps in all. All of the regulars have their favorite drinks and aren't shy about sharing their opinions. Here are my thoughts on just some of the items you'll find here.

WATER, TEA, AND CAF

The bar imports **Kamino Rain** water (still or sparkling). Looking for more flavor than that? Try the tea and caf selections. The hearty hot drink of the locals, **Spiran Caf**, is grown and roasted in the foothills of the mountains that stretch across Batuu. Like other varieties of caf served in diners throughout the galaxy, it will provide you a nice kick of energy. Try its richer variant, **Black Spire Brew**, if you prefer something sweet and cold. Imported all the way from Mandalore, **Cassius Tea** is made with the florets of the cassius tree and thought to be good for your health. Try the well-garnished **Moogan Tea** or the **Tarine Tea**, rumored to be a favorite of the First Order. If you prefer a sweet tea with a bit of a crunch, you'll like the **Sweet Root Tea**.

NON-ALCOHOLIC LIBATIONS

Some travelers are surprised to find a cloud of smoke rolling out of the **Carbon Freeze**, which is far more enjoyable than actually being frozen in carbonite and comes with none of the carbon sickness afterward. Using the same locally farmed milk as the Milk Stand, the **Blue Bantha** served at Oga's Cantina is topped with a special sweet snack. The **Felucian Fizz** is a real crowd-pleaser on a hot day. Some say the concoction helps fight dehydration. The **Blurrgfire** can be found at taverns and cantinas across the galaxy, but Oga puts her own twist on this classic stand by. And if you want to sip on a regional favorite, try a **Cliff Dweller**, which is a deep orange color and big on flavor.

COCKTAILS

Yellow, fruity, and topped with foam, the **Fuzzy Tauntaun** is served cold as Hoth and lovingly named after the snow lizard creatures who live there. The **Yub Nub** (Ewokese for "freedom") is my favorite cocktail on the menu. Complete with seeds from fruit imported directly from Endor, the drink conjures up memories of my own travels to the world of the Ewoks. The shimmering **Bespin Fizz** is aptly named and will fizz and bubble while you drink it. The **Jedi Mind Trick** doesn't require the Force to enjoy, but might leave you a bit bewildered how it changes flavor as you drink it.

WINE

For something light and refreshing, try the **Andoan White** imported from the planet Ando, home of the Aqualish species. This thirst-quenching white wine is crisp and balanced. Produced for generations on the ship-building planet for which it is named, **Corellian Red** is stocked to please the ship-faring crowd. Smugglers, shipbuilders, and freighter pilots alike find comfort in this old favorite. The **Imperial Guard**, like the old Galactic Empire, is bold and robust. I recommend the **Toniray Wine**, a bubbly teal-colored varietal made famous on the planet Alderaan. Since the planet's destruction more than thirty years ago, this vintage is exceedingly rare.

BEER & CIDER

The **Bad Motivator IPA** is one of the most flavorful beers on tap. Silky smooth and most refreshing on warm days, the **White Wampa Ale** is my personal favorite. Speaking of favorites, local business owner Hondo Ohnaka is quick to recommend the **Gamorrean Ale**. Those looking for a lighter option should try the **Gold Squadron Lager**. Cider fans will find the **Spice Runner**, a dark red drink named in honor of the spice smugglers who keep so busy in this corner of the galaxy.

Don't try to walk out with a full glass. Oga dislikes many things and stolen glassware is certainly one of them. She's also weary that competing bartenders might try to replicate her specialty cocktails. In either case, Oga's not taking any chances.

DJ R-3X

Experienced travelers from the days of the Galactic Empire might recognize the droid playing DJ at the Cantina. RX-series droids like this one once served in the travel and leisure industry, playing hosts aboard civilian transport ships that regularly crossed the hyperspace lanes. One such operation was the fledgling tour firm known as **Star Tours**, which served myriad destinations with a fleet of **Starspeeder 3000** starships. **RX-24** was just one of the pilot droids pressed into service until a fateful voyage led the hapless droid and his passengers right into a battle between the Rebel Alliance and Imperial Navy. Luckily, no one was hurt in the ordeal but the embarrassing affair meant RX-24 was out of a job.

Since his time at Star Tours, RX-24 claims to have held many jobs. He talks of his days piloting ferry shuttles from Garel before eventually joining the Rebel Alliance as a cargo pilot. He insists he was part of the Battle of Jakku, the pivotal battle that finally ended the Galactic Civil War. All we know for certain is that the little droid found himself here on Batuu. Thanks to the local droid expert Mubo, RX-24's programming was altered to turn the former pilot into a DJ, spinning music and entertaining the crowds who pack Oga's Cantina. The droid, now known as DJ R-3X, is the latest addition to Oga's Cantina.

THE PEOPLE: OGA'S CANTINA

The staff under Oga's employ are no strangers to dealing with sketchy clientele and the trouble they bring with them. Legend tells that the Imperial enforcer, Darth Vader, even passed through this door more than forty years ago. They've seen and heard it all and know how to deal with the worst. Yet when they aren't breaking up brawls between customers, their real talents in mixology shine. Oga's attracts visitors from all around the galaxy and the bartenders at Oga's always seem to find the perfect drink to match any palate.

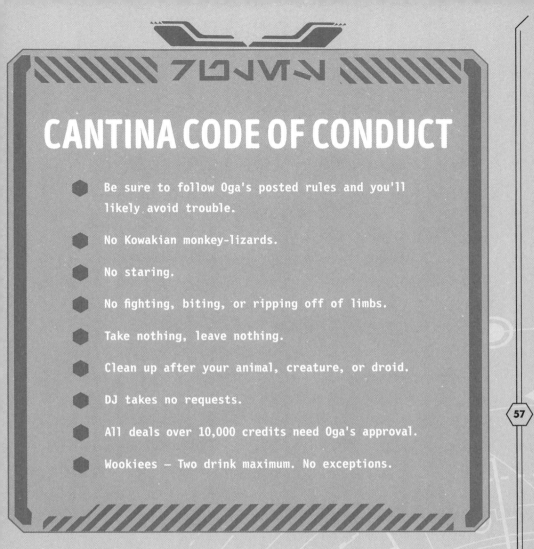

CANTINA CODE OF CONDUCT

- Be sure to follow Oga's posted rules and you'll likely avoid trouble.

- No Kowakian monkey-lizards.

- No staring.

- No fighting, biting, or ripping off of limbs.

- Take nothing, leave nothing.

- Clean up after your animal, creature, or droid.

- DJ takes no requests.

- All deals over 10,000 credits need Oga's approval.

- Wookiees — Two drink maximum. No exceptions.

While the rule about **Wookiees** might strike you as odd, it's almost certainly because of Oga's long history with members of the hairy species. Her most recent boyfriend, a Wookiee named **Dhoran**, made the mistake of cheating on Oga with a Rodian. She blasted him just outside the Cantina, sending him tumbling over a railing that still stands unrepaired outside the establishment to this day.

For a decade, the highest authority in the Cantina was Oga. Her word was final in all matters, whether personal disagreements or big business deals. In recent days, stormtroopers of the **First Order** have started stopping into the Cantina with increased frequency. It's the kind of attention that Oga doesn't want in her establishment. If questioned, you'll do well to answer their inquiries. For more on the First Order, see page 78.

CANTINA CREATURES

Travelers often ask me about the strange creatures Oga keeps in her Cantina. No, I'm not talking about the clientele; I'm referring to the ones she keeps behind the bar. In fact, these creatures are hard at work providing key ingredients for some of Oga's most exquisite concoctions.

The **mynocks** hanging there might be a cause for concern for starship pilots. After all, these flying parasites are best known for chewing on power cables of ships traveling through space. But on the planet Ryloth, they serve as a delicacy for Twi'leks who cook them into a spicy dish. Oga's staff keep pickled mynock on hand as an ingredient in drinks, adding a unique zest that brings out the flavors of the other ingredients.

Also found in the cantina is the Taozin grub. This topshelf grub is reserved only for Oga's most VIP guests. The grub's brine is an exotic and valuable delicacy to some species who believe it gives them mental fortitude. The liquid is life-preserving and sedating for the grub as it infuses the liquid with certain qualities. It's most likely why the crime lord Dryden Vos kept one handy in his yacht.

TAOZIN GRUB

The **swamp slugs** here came all the way from the swamp planet of Dagobah. As a rule, you wouldn't want to come face to face with one of these creatures. In the wild, they use the thousands of tiny teeth that line their esophagi to grind up plants and animals they eat. They excrete a distinct slime from their bodies, which has become quite valuable for cooks and mixologists. One specialty cocktail here, the Dagobah Slug Slinger, uses the slime of the swamp slug as a key ingredient.

Far from its native habitat on the sandy planet of Tatooine, a **worrt** now calls Oga's Cantina its home. Normally, you might find one of these creatures burrowed in the sand waiting for prey to pass before snatching it up with its lightning-fast tongue. The worrt here lays hundreds of eggs each day, a critical ingredient in some cantina drinks. They're a delicacy that I encourage you to try at least once, but do be cautious around the creature's tongue.

WORRT

SERVICE YARD

Though it's just one of the many back alleys that connect the streets here, the **service yard** near merchant row is a notable example. Once home to the outpost's public baths, it is now a public refresher. They're outfitted with facilities for most humanoid species.

Taking a quick stroll around the yard, visitors will notice a droid repair station. On any given day it's bustling with activity as astromechs and other such automatons wait in line for repairs or perhaps just a soothing oil bath. There is also a rather large Imperial probe droid, captured by local Batuuans many decades ago during the time of the Galactic Empire, hanging on a wall for all see.

The service yard is just one of many places around town where you can hear the local radio station, **BSO 401.72.** The station's DJ, **Palob Godalhi,** is the closest thing Black Spire has to a local celebrity. Stick around a while to hear the latest news, some favorite music, and more.

DOK-ONDAR'S DEN OF ANTIQUITIES

For a hundred years, **Dok-Ondar** and his infamous **Den of Antiquities** has been one of Black Spire Outposts most visited destinations. Dok, as he's known to the locals, is one of the galaxy's premiere collectors of artifacts and curiosities. While he has clients around the Outer Rim and beyond, this shop is his headquarters. His fame as a historian and merchant means that he no longer has to scour the galaxy for new items one at a time. Instead, beings come from far and wide to bring him their latest finds, hoping to learn more about their treasures and sell them to Dok who is known to pay substantial sums for truly remarkable finds. In turn, the enterprising Ithorian sells them in his shop or to a short list of exclusive clients.

Just outside the front door, you will already find some of Dok's impressive collection, some of a mysteriously spiritual origin. Crates filled with unique relics not only entice visitors to step inside, they suggest that Dok's store is so full of antiquities that his magnificent shop simply cannot contain them all.

Native to the planet Ithor, the Ithorians are perhaps best known for being peaceful horticulturists. They have expanded throughout the galaxy over the eons, and many have put their gardening past behind them. They have two mouths but are unable to vocalize the sounds required to speak Basic. They rely on translators to speak with most other species.

As you approach Dok-Ondar's Den of Antiquities, you'll find a large stone **totem**. This hand-carved relic has great spiritual meaning on Dok's home planet of Ithor, where it was once the marker for his parents' grave. It's one of the few reminders of Dok's life prior to Batuu, before he was the famous Dok-Ondar.

LOOK INSIDE: DOK-ONDAR'S DEN OF ANTIQUITIES

When you step inside Dok-Ondar's shop, take a moment to appreciate the **mural** that hangs before you. The frieze depicts a long-forgotten battle between good and evil. Warriors with ancient swords and shields clash as war beasts charge into the fray. Give yourself time to ponder, *Which side is good and which side is evil?* It's said that during the days of the Republic, Supreme Chancellor Palpatine (later named Emperor) had a similar mural in his office likely created by the same artist.

Move farther inside and you'll find the main chamber filled with Dok's most valuable items. Dok-Ondar himself works from his perch on the other side of the room and is here more often than not. He keeps a busy schedule overseeing the shop's affairs, closely inspecting items, cataloguing new acquisitions, updating his meticulous bookkeeping, and talking with his staff of **apprentices**. Between them, they know where every single item is located.

Looking up, you'll see **Ithorian weather chimes**, handmade on Ithor to pray for fertile soil and good weather for gardening. More chimes adorn his counter, serving as a reminder of the home planet Dok left so long ago. Elsewhere, you might spot an original mask worn by **General Grievous**. The Kaleesh warlord gained galactic infamy for his role leading the Separatist droid army during the Clone Wars a half century ago. The general had many such masks on hand, ready to replace battle-damaged parts of his cyborg body.

Jedi and Sith artifacts are some of Dok-Ondar's specialties and he has decades of experience identifying the very best examples. Busts and statues are well sought after, especially those that feature famous members of the Jedi Council. Ancient Jedi and Sith texts sometimes pass through the shop as well. Collectors should keep an eye out for statues of the **Four Sages of Dwartii**——Sistros, Braata, Faya, and Yanjun——the ancient philosophers and lawmakers who influenced the earliest laws in the Galactic Republic.

Imperial artifacts became quite popular in recent decades. Collectors—many of whom are too young to have lived during Imperial rule—take great interest in the uniforms, armor, and adornments of the old Empire. As memory of the Emperor fades, these collectors relish the opportunity to own something that he created.

KALEESH
MASK

DOK-ONDAR & HIS APPRENTICES

A collector of all things odd, curious and antiquated, **Dok-Ondar** is Black Spire Outpost's most distinguished and infamous resident. His collection of rare and one-of-a-kind items is unrivaled thanks to his shrewd business practices, a keen eye for the extraordinary, and expert negotiation skills. In this haven for smugglers and the black market, Dok is the gatekeeper.

I'm told that Dok-Ondar wasn't always a domineering figure. Born to a family of gardeners, Dok grew up finding unusual rocks, bones, and other curiosities while gardening. As he grew up, his family encouraged his collection and allowed him to develop the skills he needed to buy, sell, and trade for a living. After the sudden death of his parents, Dok came to Batuu. Some say he is still seeking answers about his own past.

Dok-Ondar is more than 240 years old and the charms he wears around his neck exemplify just some of the many places he has been and people he has met. A few of the charms look like fingers and have sparked debate around the Outpost. Did their owners give them to Dok to prove their loyalty or did he take them from dishonest pirates and smugglers? It's just one of the many mysteries that surround one of Black Spire Outpost's oldest residents.

What is clear is that Dok-Ondar is both feared and respected on Batuu and beyond. Anyone who attempts to cheat the old Ithorian will find a bounty on their head. His list of enemies is known to locals as the "Doklist," and you don't want to be on it. Instead, it's much better to be on Dok's good side. The nature of Dok's business requires him to maintain a list of wealthy clients. Dok makes it a priority to keep these customers happy, taking their calls personally. You'll need to spend often and in large amounts if you want to make it on this exclusive list reserved for the galaxy's most discerning collectors such as Hiro the Hutt, Zep Sulgo, and Ve-Ta Naswee.

Across Black Spire Outpost, Dok employs a trusted team to carry out his business. **Tohago** is his right-hand woman who handles his day-to-day operations, often representing him at the spaceport to oversee his flow of goods that pass through the planet. She speaks multiple languages and serves as Dok's translator as well. When the situation calls for brute force, Dok calls on the Clawdite, **Varg**. For almost thirty years, this former bounty hunter has been Dok's muscle. His species' ability to shapeshift proves to be quite useful when dealing with dangerous clientele. As deadly as he is loyal, IG-series assassin droid **BK-86** serves as Dok's security, protecting his master when deals go sour. Client service in his shop rests with a hand-picked group of **antiquarian apprentices**. While charming, they can be somewhat aggressive when closing a deal on black market items.

As the Outpost's most successful entrepreneur, he has taken on the unofficial role as town banker, keeping tabs on the debts owed to him and Oga. He keeps the books, while Oga provides the muscle needed to keep trade flowing through the outpost. Dok's sizable abacus helps him keep track of debts and calculate big-ticket deals.

IG DROID

DOK-ONDAR'S CREATURES & TAXIDERMY

Dok's interests don't end with mysterious relics. He also appreciates items from the natural world. The galaxy teems with interesting life-forms and Dok's collection of living and taxidermic creatures is among the best in this part of the galaxy. Some specimens he finds himself during his travels, while others are brought to him in trade or as payment.

Dok keeps a number of taxidermy busts on hand as well. The fierce **anooba** is a pack predator and is prized for its ability to be trained. The four-eyed **nexu** have infrared vision and are great climbers on their homeworld of Cholganna. **Tauntauns** from Hoth are prey for the carnivorous wampas and are known to emit a strong odor. **Kod'yoks** are native to Vandor, where they are valued for their fur, meat, and skins.

WAMPA

This taxidermic wampa from the planet Hoth was a gift from Kasif, a Trandoshan hunter friend.

SARLACC

This sarlacc named Simpi is but a juvenile. Fully grown specimens grow more than one hundred meters long. This display provides a fine overview of how the creatures burrow into sand and wait for prey to fall into their gaping maw. Locals brag that this sarlacc is the specimen brought to the Outpost by famed smugglers Han Solo and Chewbacca.

FELUCIAN FIREFLIES

Dok collected these beautiful bugs on a trip to Felucia, a planet known for its colorful array of flora.

DIANOGA

Another juvenile example of a species, this dianoga is named Toothy. Dianogas, native to the planet Vodran, are known to have regenerative tentacles that grow back if lost. Dok bought this diangoa from Jabba the Hutt as part of a deal.

SIBIAN HOUND

Native to the planet Corellia, Sibian Hounds have been bred to be attack dogs for generations. They are particularly vicious and highly effective hunters, which makes outwitting one a prize worthy to display.

OLLOPOM

Nicknamed Ollie, this Ollopom is a rodent from Naboo's Gungan swamps. It's distinctive hair and fur helps it blend in with the aquatic pom petal plants that they live among and feed upon.

ANOOBA

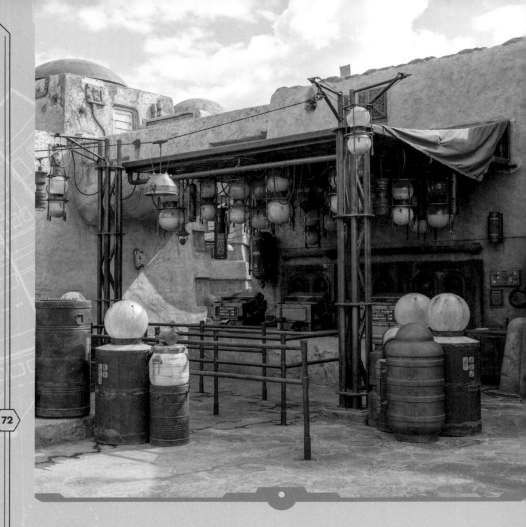

MILK STAND

Four Generations of the **Wamba family** have kept banthas on their farm on Tatooine. Their modest operations expanded in recent years to include a farm, just a short distance outside of Black Spire Outpost. After years of working for his parents on Tatooine, the young Aqualish **Bubo Wamba** now runs the family's farm and has opened a milk stand selling local and imported milk to the many travelers who pass through the Outpost.

Like you and I, Bubo is absolutely fascinated by the wonderful mix of cultures here on Black Spire. He comes from a small town—if you can even call it that—and it shows. Though he spends much of his time on the farm tending to the banthas, he takes every opportunity to meet new people from across the galaxy.

The **Wamba Family Farm's Milk Stand** is highly recommended. If you're looking for a refreshing, nutritious beverage, I think you can't go wrong with any of the varieties here. It's extraordinary to find blue milk so fresh from the source. Knowing that the beverage you're drinking was milked just steps from where you stand is a real treat. It's even more rare to get to try the green milk harvested from thala-sirens, creatures less commonly seen across the galaxy. Assisting Bubo in the day-to-day sales are a small group of helpful **milk vendors**. They do one thing, but they do it well: milk! Don't hesitate to ask the quirky staff questions about where they sourced your drink or how fresh the drinks are today.

AROUND THE GALAXY: BANTHAS

Banthas are furry mammals that travel in herds and are kept by ranchers in nearly every corner of the galaxy. On Bubo Wamba's home planet of Tatooine, bantha farmers manage their herds without the need for fences, letting their animals roam the sand dunes that cover so much of the planet. Their distinct blue milk is an important source of nutrition for the farming families of Tatooine. Other local inhabitants, the Tusken Raiders, keep banthas as mounts.

DOCKING BAY 9

DOCKING BAY 9

Until very recently, **Docking Bay 9** was just another place to park your starship. Like other docking bays in this area, it primarily served local shuttles. Now, however, the status quo has been upset by the arrival of the **First Order**. This once-quiet corner of the Outpost now teems with activity. The sounds of boots marching in unison fills the air. The quiet chatter of Batuuans has been replaced with the electronic voices of stormtroopers. Flags of the First Order fly proudly nearby. If you appreciate displays of power and precision, you'll find a lot in common with these new occupants.

 The First Order doesn't look to be leaving anytime soon. They've commandeered the landing platform as well as the nearby loading bay and storage dock. The sheer amount of materiel they've brought down to the planet is impressive and perhaps that's the point. This base of operations also serves as their recruiting headquarters and quite a few local Batuuans have been captivated by the display.

 Officers and enlisted troops alike all focus on one common cause: locating the Resistance. If you find yourself in this corner of the Outpost, don't be surprised if you get questioned about what—and who—you know.

TIE ECHELON: TECHNICAL FILE

The First Order's TIE echelon is now a regular sight in Docking Bay 9. The shuttle ferries officers, troops, dignitaries, and supplies from the orbiting Star Destroyer to the outpost. It is surprisingly well armed for a craft of its size, boasting weapon systems and advanced sensors that outclass almost any other shuttle that visits the outpost. Some locals claim that its arrival is nothing to worry about, while others are concerned by this obvious show of force

Manufacturer: Sienar-Jaemus Fleet Systems
Model: TIE echelon
Type: Assault shuttle
Class: Transport
Crew: 1-2 pilots
Passengers: 10
Cargo Capacity: 20 metric tons
Armament: 4 heavy laser cannons,
1 dual cannon turret

HEAVY LASER CANNON

SOLAR ENERGY COLLECTORS

SOLAR POWER CONVERTER

SENSOR ARRAY

COMMUNICATIONS ANTENNA

DUAL CANNON TURRET

DEFLECTOR SHIELD GENERATOR

THE PEOPLE: THE FIRST ORDER

Officers in pristine, finely tailored uniforms oversee the detachment of stormtroopers deployed on Batuu. One such leader, **First Lieutenant Agnon** joined the First Order at a young age and is a staunch believer in its cause. He and his fellow First Order officers value order and strength above all else. Since there is not government in the Outpost to work with directly, it's up to these officers to be diplomatic in their relations with the various personalities in town.

The First Order's arrival has already inspired local Batuuans to rally to their cause. These **loyalists** aren't officially part of the First Order, but aid the organization here in town. If you've seen some of the rougher parts of Batuu, you can begin to understand the allure of the First Order. Some here have known only lawlessness their whole lives. The First Order promises to bring galactic peace through absolute order. The thought of having protection and a higher purpose gives these loyalists hope that the future will be brighter.

Nicknamed the **Red Fury**, the troopers of Supreme Leader Kylo Ren's **709th Legion** are an impressive sight to behold. Like many troopers in the First Order, most of them were trained since birth to be soldiers. The only life they've ever known is military service and they have no desire to leave. I've spoken with many loyalists who dream of joining their ranks someday soon, if only they can prove themselves worthy of this elite unit.

STORMTROOPER

STORMTROOPER OFFICER

PRISONER CONTROL STORMTROOPER

When there's a need for extra support during social unrest, prisoner control stormtroopers are called in to assist. Their electroprod is far from lethal, but provides enough force to ensure compliance.

TIE FIGHTER PILOT

These troops specialize in flying agile fighter craft. They are rarely seen outside of their starfighters or capital ships. Rumors persist that some TIE fighter pilots have never set foot on a planet, having been raised and trained aboard starships.

FLAMETROOPER

These soldiers are a fearsome addition to the First Order ranks. They wield powerful flame throwers fueled by tanks worn upon their backs. They can decimate encampments or clear out bunkers with the pull of a trigger.

SNOWTROOPER

Proof that the First Order operates in a wide range of environments, snowtrooper armor provides advantages in colder climates. Their narrow eye shield prevents glare off of frozen surfaces. Quilted coverings provide increased comfort for the troops, allowing them to remain operational for longer periods.

FLEET GUNNER

More lightly armored than ground troops, these gunners have more flexibility when operating heavy equipment and gunnery stations. Their helmets are specially designed to provide targeting information.

EXECUTIONER TROOPER

In the First Order, disloyalty is not allowed and traitors are dealt with swiftly. When handing down punishments, a First Order executioner trooper is rarely far behind. These stormtroopers wield laser axes to carry out their grim orders.

FIRST ORDER MILITARY

Until recently, few realized the scale of mechanical might the First Order possessed. Reports of their full capabilities have since flooded the HoloNet, shocking military analysts. Their armies might be modeled after the Galactic Empire of old, but their forces represent the latest in military technology.

UPSILON-CLASS COMMAND SHUTTLE

A transport of choice for the First Order's highest-ranking members. Shield generators and state-of-the-art sensor jamming technology help protect these leading figures.

XI-CLASS LIGHT SHUTTLE

Lightly armed and armored, this shuttle is most often accompanied by a fighter escort.

ALL TERRAIN SCOUT TRANSPORT

The First Order's AT-ST is a nimble walker for ground operations that boasts next-generation composite armor.

ALL TERRAIN ARMORED TRANSPORT

Standing tall upon four stout legs, the twenty-two-meter-tall AT-AT holds up to forty passengers. They are ferried through space in Star Destroyers, ready for invasion.

TIE/SF SPACE SUPERIORITY FIGHTER

The fighter of choice for the First Order's special forces, this two-seater variant of the TIE is equipped with a hyperdrive for long-range missions.

RESURGENT-CLASS STAR DESTROYER

With turbolasers powered by kyber crystals, these modern Star Destroyers are more efficient and capable than their predecessors. Each boasts thousands of ground troops and two wings of starfighters.

MANDATOR IV-CLASS SIEGE DREADNOUGHT

This massive platform is designed to blast planetary targets from space using dual orbital bombardment cannons.

TIE/FO SPACE SUPERIORITY FIGHTER

Swarms of TIE fighters once again fill the skies as the First Order advances across the galaxy. Fast and deadly, this is the most common starfighter in the fleet.

FIRST ORDER PROPAGANDA

Like the Empire that came before it, the First Order embraces the power of propaganda to spread their message and encourage others to join their ranks. These are just some examples of the persuasive art you might encounter during this tumultuous time in the galaxy.

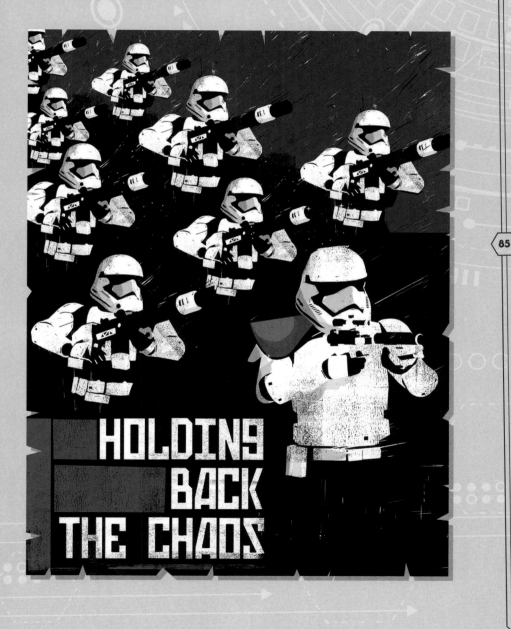

THE SPACEPORT

THE SPACEPORT

A bustling center of activity, the **Black Spire Outpost Spaceport** invites off-worlders into the very heart of the city. Its far more than just a place to park a starship; it's a jumping-off point to all that the Outpost has to offer. Landing here puts you just steps away from the all-important local cantina or a short walk to the lively market.

The spaceport's many landing bays are the most convenient place on the planet for handling cargo, taking on supplies, and acquiring starship repairs. Standing tall above it all is the **flight tower**, staffed day and night to direct all incoming and departing port traffic. On the ground, local Batuuans can help you find almost anything you require. Most work directly for local boss Oga Garra, and they're also quick to collect landing fees as her representative. While bribes might work in other places, the crews here know not to short change Oga, so don't bother trying to buy your way out of trouble. If you are the captain of a starship looking to put together a crew, here you will also find all forms of skilled (and unskilled) personnel looking for work.

Spaceport bays can be leased directly from Oga Garra. One business to recently move into the spaceport is **Ohnaka Transport Solutions**, a shipping outfit that has begun to attract the attention of people looking for work. The man behind it all is none other than Captain **Hondo Ohnaka**. He claims his new business is 100 percent legitimate, but Hondo's own record suggests that things might not always be on the up-and-up. His reputation as a scoundrel (or worse) has followed him here to the Outpost and he's already getting mixed reviews. For pilots looking for work on this far-flung outpost, however, Hondo's offer might just be too good to pass up. He himself is quick to assure me, "When Hondo profits, so do you." And though I've heard otherwise, he guarantees all of his associates, "Hondo always delivers!" I know from experience though that he doesn't always pick up his tab, and I was left paying for his drinks at the local cantina after our first meeting.

HONDO OHNAKA

Hondo Ohnaka was once the captain of a gang of Weequay pirates based on the planet Florrum. They gained some amount of fame a half century ago, taking full advantage of the chaos created by the Clone Wars to run amok in the Outer Rim and run a salvage operation on the side. Their years of plunder ended after an entanglement with the Empire, forcing Hondo to partner with a variety of dodgy beings, some of whom lived to tell a cautionary tale of their misadventures alongside the infamous pirate. Rumors suggest he has kept company with bounty hunters, smugglers, rebels, and even Jedi throughout his many years.

Hondo's fleet of vessels now includes the famed *Millennium Falcon*, which must be in truly desperate need of repairs for it to fall into the hands of a pirate like Hondo. Like so many others, he has long sought this opportunity to possess such a storied ship.

THE *MILLENNIUM FALCON:* TECHNICAL FILE

Manufacturer: Corellian Engineering Corporation
Model: YT-1300
Type: Light freighter (heavily modified)
Class: Transport
Crew: 2 (minimum)
Cargo Capacity: 100 metric tons
Armament: 2 CEC AG-2G quad laser cannons, 2 Arakyd ST2 concussion missile tubes, 1 BlasTech Ax-108 "ground buzzer" blaster cannon

DURALLOY PLATING

WARP VORTEX STABILIZER

MAIN ACCESS BAY

DEFLECTOR SHIELD PROJECTOR

TEMPORARY MAIN SENSOR RECTENNA

FORWARD FLOODLIGHT

HYPERSPACE INTEGRATOR

CUNCUSSION MISSILE

DEGAUSSER

QUAD LASER CANNON (UPPER)

STARBOARD DOCKING RING

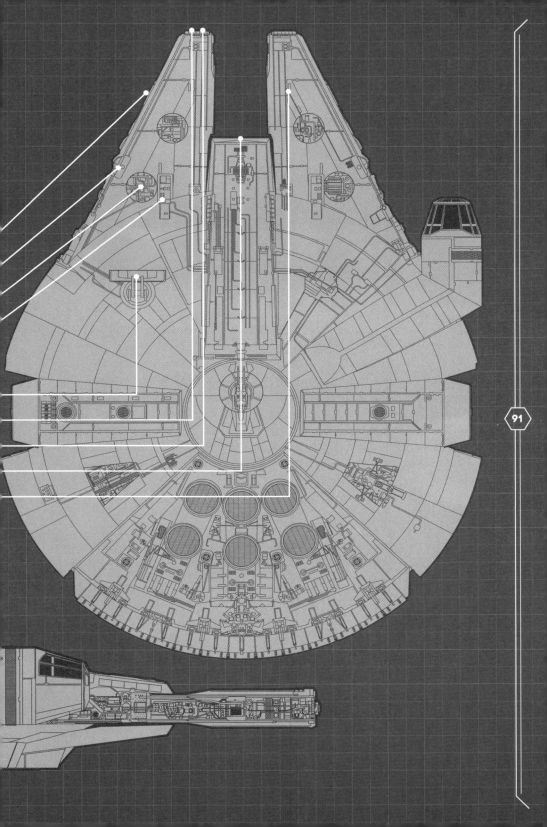

BOUNTY HUNTERS

While some who come here want to keep a low profile and make a new start, they may find they cannot escape their past mistakes. **Bounty hunters** know Batuu as a place to find those who wish not to be found. It's nothing personal; after all, the bounty hunters are just doing their job. Here in the Outpost, finding work is often as simple as stopping in the local cantina. That's where bounties are offered and information on targets is gleaned from the local gossip. Getting someone to talk usually just requires buying them a few drinks or paying a simple bribe to improve their memory.

Black Spire Outpost has seen some of the galaxy's most notorious bounty hunters walk down its streets. Batuuans speak of the vicious Nikto named **Harkos**, who has been seen here before. Bounty hunters with his skills have no need to take small jobs. He is only motivated by the most high-profile targets and the most influential buyers.

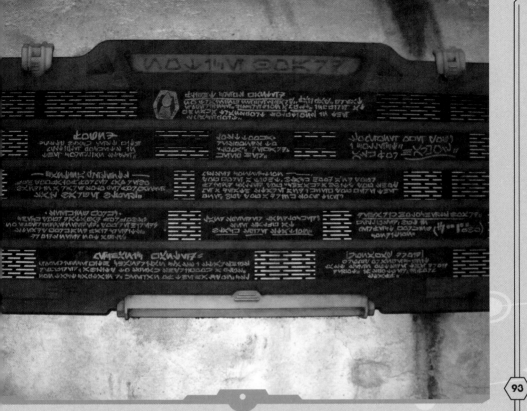

Word travels quickly here on Batuu. If you make trouble, locals are going to hear about it. If you find yourself on anyone's bad list, you'd be well advised to do whatever it takes to get yourself off of it. Actions speak louder than words, so taking a new job to repay your debts is one option to consider. Slicing into the local computers to remove your name entirely is another route you could take, but that's a risky operation best undertaken by tech-savvy slicers. Never forget what the locals say: "You've got nothing but your reputation here. The Spire always remembers."

THE MARKET

THE MARKET

The largest and most vibrant market on all of Batuu can be found right here at Black Spire Outpost. An explosion of color, sounds, and smells welcome you to one of the busiest hubs of daily life here in the Outpost. Multicolor tarps hang over head to keep out the elements as traders show off their wares. The mess of latticework and disorderly wires strung overhead is a perfect reflection of the organized chaos you'll find here. The smell of cooked grains waft through the streets as the laughs of Kowakian monkey-lizards echo down the narrow lane.

Every centimeter of this bustling market is valuable space. While shops occupy the lower levels, apartments perch above to provide housing for Black Spire residents. When the suns set, an array of lamps spark to life to illuminate the pathways and envelop the whole space in a warm glow that invites the weary traveler.

This market offers the widest variety of wares found on Batuu. Whether you seek a new pet, a fun toy, new clothes, fine jewelry, or even just a savory snack, you'll find it here. There's always something new to see at the market, encouraging visitors to return time and again.

CREATURE STALL

From frightening fyrnocks to cuddly convorees, the **Creature Stall** gathers animals from across the galaxy right here in the market of Black Spire Outpost. **Porgs** are a recent addition, brought to the planet aboard a light freighter that arrived through the spaceport. These birds show a real ability to adapt to their new surroundings and their inquisitive nature makes them friendly to most beings.

Bina, an Amani from the planet Utapau, opened this stall as a sort of home base for her exotic creature collecting. While most of her tribal people are known as warriors, Bina's interest lies in exploration and adventure. She is rarely home here in Black Spire, her travels taking from one interesting planet to another in search of ever more curious finds. Yet even when she is gone, her style is present throughout her store. Staves, ropes, blankets, and other decorations that adorn the shop represent her culture and heritage. It's one of the few times you will be able to get a taste of Amani culture outside of their secretive nomadic camps on the plains of Utapau.

If you're looking to purchase a creature, a variety of species are available here. Bina employs a small group of **creature assistants** to assist you in selecting the right animal. For your safety and for the safety of the creature, the assistants will only offer you species that fit your lifestyle. Not everyone is cut out to own a rancor, after all!

Around the corner from the stall, Bina keeps her overflow inventory of **Kowakian monkey-lizards**. I've never seen such an array of colors and patterns as she has amassed. Yet no matter what they look like, they are undoubtedly pure-bred specimens. Their distinctive laughs are unmistakable and their sense of humor is quite advanced for an animal species. When purchasing a Kowakian, only buy from a reputable seller who knows the difference between a Kowakian monkey-lizard and a Kowakian monkey-ape. The two appear quite similar, but are completely different in temperament and size. It's possible to mistake a juvenile ape for a full-grown lizard. The unsuspecting owner is sure in for a surprise when the young ape grows to be larger than a human!

JEWELS OF BITH

Looking for a souvenir from your visit to Batuu? A perennial favorite is the **Jewels of Bith**. In this tiny market stall, you'll find the perfect "trinket to treasure" from Black Spire. While it offers scarves and other accessories as well, it's best known for the little treasures crafted by proprietor **Kamka Lira**. You'll be impressed by the ingenuity she displays as a designer, forging unique items out of almost any material. Whether you have modest means or unlimited credits, you'll find something that fits within your budget.

Kamka is also a seasoned traveler, bringing back items from far-off planets and some of the galaxy's top designers. She curates an impressive collection for sale to discerning customers. If Kamka is not available when you call, her team can assist you with any question.

THE WOODEN WOOKIEE

The gifted Wookiee woodcarver **Lunacca** shares his talents with Black Spire at his shop tucked away in the market. Fittingly named **The Wooden Wookiee**, here you will find everything from small trinkets to large sculptures made from hardwoods gathered on his homeworld of Kashyyyk. Many of the wooden vessels used to serve drinks in town are made right here. As you pass by, take a moment to admire the hand-carved Wookiee war shields made nearly indestructible using the sap of the wroshyr tree.

Lunacca makes frequent trips back to his home in search of supplies, leaving his shop closed during his journeys. This stall is a one-Wookiee operation, and unlike some of the other vendors, he doesn't employ locals to help with customer service in his absence. Most who live on Batuu lack the strength to whittle wroshyr, so you can be guaranteed that every item here was created by his hands.

AROUND THE GALAXY: WOOKIEES

Proud and noble, the Wookiees of Kashyyyk faced hard times throughout recent galactic history. Their forested homeworld was a battleground during the Clone Wars and then subjugated by the Empire. Many Wookiees were forced into slavery until they were freed by the New Republic shortly after the Battle of Endor. Today, they live a largely peaceful existence, sharing their love for the natural world with those who visit. The forests are making a remarkable comeback from the deforestation campaign carried out by the Empire.

BLACK SPIRE OUTFITTERS

Your best bet for a new outfit in the Outpost comes from **Black Spire Outfitters**, a classically styled clothing store in the market. The shop is bursting with color, welcoming you to shop for your next outfit.

Arta and her staff of **clothiers** are as helpful as they come. Never pushy, they just want to make sure you find the outfit that is right for you. Look closely at some of the custom pieces hanging in the shop and you'll see that Arta has an impressive client list, earned thanks to her relentless focus on quality, comfort, and function. To keep up with demand, Arta employs the help of a sewing assistant droid, **GX-8**. Every one of its many arms is specially designed for mending and sewing garments.

Arta continues to offer traditionally styled robes and tabards, while they might not be considered high fashion today, her patterns harken back to the designs worn before the Galactic Civil War, a time where flowing, hooded robes were much more common. The matching belts and pouches are perfect for travelers even today.

Like so many of the merchants here, they offer handmade items you won't find anywhere else. The sewing supplies, spools of thread, and in-progress garments are proof that these pieces were made with care by the classically styled Twi'lek **Arta Kleidun**. She doesn't get distracted by the latest fashions of the core worlds. Instead, she carries on the rich tradition of crafting timeless pieces that are made to last a lifetime. Rather than build a flashy showroom, Arta has created a store as humble as she is.

TOYDARIAN TOYMAKER

Has there ever been a more fitting name for a market shop than **Toydarian Toymaker**? It's as if **Zabaka**, the owner and head toy maker, was born for this occupation! Whether you have a child or are a child at heart, this shop is worth a visit. Her soft toys are hand sewn, the metal games are personally welded with care, and her puppets are carved with love. With such a wide selection of toys for sale, Zabaka stays quite busy, rarely taking a break from her office workshop. The shop is also her home, as you can see by the nest in the corner of her stall. It's all work and no play for this busy entrepreneur.

Zabaka seems to find inspiration from the people and objects all around her. Her toys, particularly the stuffed varieties, are exceedingly popular with younglings. I've even met a few adult fans of her work. Perhaps as the result of living in a rough corner of the galaxy, even a hardened smuggler needs something to take their mind off business.

For the musically inclined, Toydarian Toymaker is just about the only place on the entire planet to find musical instruments for sale. They offer a small selection of the more common instruments made famous by star musicians, but you will have to look off-world for regional variants or bring your own culture's specialty with you.

Since opening more than five years ago, Zabaka's business has really taken flight. To keep up with demand, she now employs knowledgeable **apprentices** who can help you make informed purchases. However, the quality of the toys makes it easy to look past the shortcomings of the inexperienced help.

AROUND THE GALAXY: TOYDARIA

Deep in Hutt Space, a long-standing monarchy rules the planet Toydaria. During the Clone Wars, Toydaria suffered from being caught in the middle of galactic politics. The planet has largely recovered, but its people remain wary of outside influences. Toydarians have a reputation for being shrewd business owners and are said to be immune to Force mind tricks, making them tough negotiators.

DOCKING BAY 7 FOOD & CARGO

Not far from the marketplace you will find an old hangar bay and landing platform, **Docking Bay 7**. Though it once served starship captains, today it serves hungry beings! Since Black Spire Outpost lacks a large variety of high-end restaurants, the enterprising Batuuans have come up with a clever solution. Instead of one permanent restaurant, they welcome some of the galaxy's best chefs to come here and set up a temporary dining space inside the old docking bay. The chefs stay for a while, exhibit their unique specialties, and then move on to another planet when the time is right.

Here at **Docking Bay 7 Food and Cargo**, the meals—and the chefs—arrive via food freighters. The ships are converted transports, now specially outfitted with everything a cook needs. They are a traveling kitchen, fridge, garden, warehouse, and more. While the chefs might come and go, the local Batuuan staff are permanent. The crew here are efficient but courteous, helping the guest chefs prepare food and assist travelers placing orders. After ordering, visitors are welcome to eat inside the hangar itself. Additional seating is available outside under the trees, providing a relaxing and rustic space to enjoy one's meal.

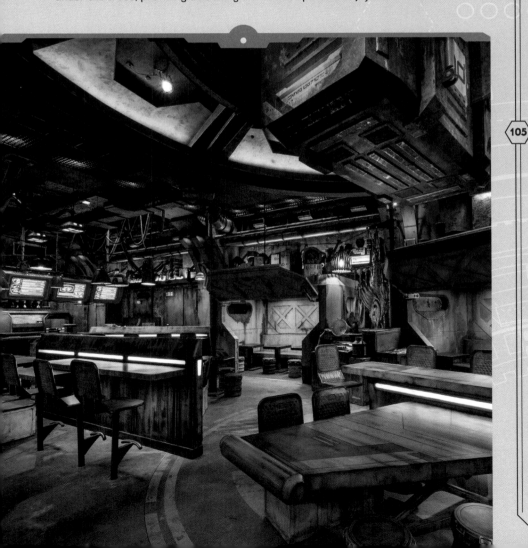

TUGGS' GRUB

The rotating guest chef serving at Docking Bay 7 Food and Cargo during my most recent visit was none other than **Strono "Cookie" Tuggs**! I've been enjoying his food for years on the planet Takodana. For centuries, he worked there under the legendary pirate Maz Kanata, serving as head chef at her castle. With the recent destruction of her famous fortress, Cookie has taken his talents on the road and Black Spire Outpost is lucky to have him!

COOKIE

He calls his new venture Tuggs' Grub, a "traveling diner for diners traveling." If you spot his modified Sienar-Chall Utilipede Transport parked atop the docking bay, you should absolutely stop for a meal before he leaves again.

Cookie's menu is always changing depending on the ingredients he has gathered on his freighter. Here are some of my recommendations from his most recent menu.

FOOD

For something a little heartier, you can't go wrong with the **Endorian Fried Chicken**. With mashed vegetables and a delectable gravy, this is easily the best preparation of the bird outside of its native home on Endor. The Tip-Yip is also

SMOKED KAADU PORK RIBS

ENDORIAN FRIED CHICKEN

served oven roasted. The **Roasted Voorpak Garden Spread** nicely balances the vegetable spread and voorpak meatballs. From the planet Naboo comes two heartier options. I enjoy the **Smoked Kaadu Pork Ribs** with tender meat topped with a sticky, smoky sauce. Hungry diners might try the **Batuuan Beef Pot Roast** served with pasta, greens, and mushrooms. Cookie only serves grass-fed Batuuan cows that graze Naboo's beautiful grasslands.

Seafood lovers should consider Cookie's marine offering. The **Surabat Shrimp and Noodle Salad** is a cool dish and one of my favorites on warm days. While the **Felucian Kefta & Hummus Garden Spread** and **Ithorian Garden Loaf** lack meat, they aren't lacking in flavor. The garden loaf is my recommendation and comes with a hearty roasted vegetable mash in a delicious mushroom sauce that comes from the nearby planet Yakork.

DRINKS

Tuggs' Grub is best known for its food, but its drink selection is surprisingly good. The **Batuubucha Tea**, fermented and bubbly, is said to have a variety of health benefits. Local Batuuans have been enjoying it for centuries but in recent years it has grown wildly popular in the core worlds among the galaxy's elite. **Moof Juice** is fruity with just a hint of a spice and served on ice. Don't confuse it with Moof milk, which is completely different. Red, cool, and refreshing, **Phattro** is one of Cookie's favorite imported beverages. Cookie occasionally even serves desserts to satisfy your sweet tooth.

KAT SAKA'S KETTLE

If you want to experience a delicious snack made of simple ingredients sourced from nearby farms, **Kat Saka's Kettle** offers locally grown grains served freshly popped in antique kettles. Their specialty is **Outpost Mix**, a sweet and salty popped grain. It's dark red and purple in color and subtly flavored with imported spices gathered from other planets. The unique fusion of spices is blended by **Kat Saka**, who personally works with spice traders and growers off-world.

For generations, the Saka family has been cultivating the land here on Batuu. **Saka Farms** was founded when Kat's great-grandparents came to Batuu as colonists generations ago. They brought with them an industrious spirit and, perhaps just as importantly, planted a crop of familiar grains. For generations, the Saka family has perfected the growing process here on Batuu. Like her grandparents and parents before her, Kat grew up working this soil and knows that her heirloom varieties are what make her popped grain mix so special.

Kat Saka's Kettle is open daily. The family hires **kettle servers** to handle sales in town, while Kat and the family run the busy operation on the family farm.

JAT KAA'S COOLERS

If you're in need of a refreshing, carbonated beverage on the go, be on the lookout for **Jat Kaa's** drink carts. The enterprising Lurmen **Jat Kaa** hails from Mygeeto but now lives on Batuu operating an imported drink business. He offers a variety of beverages served as ice cold as his home planet. R-series astromechs, purchased from Mubo the droid vendor, pilot the small carts around the outpost where they make stops outside of area businesses.

BLACK SPIRE OUTPOST OBELISK

Standing in the entrance of the market, **the Black Spire Outpost Obelisk** is an important landmark for the locals. They believe anyone who touches the obelisk and says "'Til the Spire" will be granted good luck to return safely to Black Spire again.

WATER DISPENSERS

You should keep an eye out for the market's most surprising resident: **Tiny the dianoga**. Tiny took up residence long ago inside the plumbing of the market courtyard water dispenser. I've witnessed more than one traveler gasp in surprise when they come eye to eye with Tiny.

RONTO ROASTERS

My recommendation for a hearty meal on the go is **Ronto Roasters**, the meat vendor near the Black Spire Outpost Market. This impressive restaurant is the brainchild of the butcher Bakkar. After growing up on Tatooine, he struck out on his own to bring his family's specialty—the massive **ronto**—to new customers right here on Batuu.

The most striking feature about Ronto Roasters is not the food at all. Stepping inside, travelers are met by a massive podracer engine hanging from the ceiling. Few ever get to come so close to one of these red-hot engines, but here you'll find that it serves as the establishment's cooking grill. It's the perfect centerpiece for Bakkar, a huge fan of podracing. He salvaged the engine nearby and it's a constant reminder of the sport he loves, a sport he remains loyal to even after being outlawed across the galaxy.

Bakkar employs a team of grillers and an old friend to run his shop. The pitmaster droid **8D-J8** has been by Bakkar's side since he left Tatooine. Perhaps to his disappointment, he never leaves the side of the massive grill either. The old smelter droid is reprogrammed to turn the spit and ensure the meats are cooked to perfection.

I believe the secret to the delicious ronto meat is their diet and Bakkar's family has truly perfected their care for the animals over four generations. The attention to detail shows in the food. The **Ronto Wrap** features two cuts of tender ronto meat, slaw, and Bakkar's signature **Clutch Sauce**. It's smoky, spicy, and makes this sandwich disappear faster than a podracer. The ronto's skin, which can be quite tough, has been removed entirely. The podracer engine grill has a tendency to dry out thin cuts, which Bakkar flavors into two varieties of jerky.

You'll need a drink to accompany your meal, and Ronto Roasters has you covered there too. Try the **Tatooine Sunset**, one of Bakkar's signature drinks with a touch of desert pear. Other drinks may be available seasonally.

AROUND THE GALAXY: RONTOS

Standing on four legs and sporting tall necks, rontos grow up to five meters tall. They serve as pack animals in various corners of the galaxy, hauling cargo at a plodding pace for those who can't afford skiffs or speeders.

PODRACING

Fast, dangerous, and outlawed, the sport of podracing continues to excite fans in the galaxy's Outer Rim. From the Boonta Eve Classic on Tatooine to the snowy peaks of Ando Prime, podracing continues to attract fans by the thousands to watch live races, no matter how illegal they may be. They cheer on their favorite racers, often hoping their choice would simply survive the day's race. With unstable equipment, hazardous courses, and cut throat competitors, podracing has a sinister reputation.

Podracers are all custom-built but generally feature two giant engines and a cockpit held together by cables. Racers have to pilot their craft through a series of laps, ultimately reaching the finish line and substantial prizes.

Even though it has been outlawed, you can tune in to a podrace on the local radio station BSO 401.72. The Rawani Cup is broadcast from the city of Baroonda, hosted by Bakk and Zico.

Through the years great rivalries have formed between the different racers. Arguably the greatest podracer of our generation is Sebulba. Hailing from the planet Malastare, the Dug's distinctive orange podracer struck fear into his competitors. It's generally known that humans lack the reflexes necessary to race pods, but those with extraordinary abilities are an exception. Fans on Tatooine still speak of a young human, Anakin Skywalker, winning the Boonta Eve Classic more than a half century ago.

MOS ESPA ARENA

113

AROUND THE GALAXY: PIT DROIDS

Pit droids are mechanic droids specially designed to assist in the preparation and repair of pods and other machines. Living pit crews are highly preferred to these clumsy and error-prone models. Pit droids should never be left idle. To shut them down, tap their primary receptor to put them into a convenient storage mode.

SAVI & SON SALVAGE

On the outskirts of town lies one of the Batuu's oldest businesses. **Savi and Son Salvage**, founded by the old scrapper named Savi, has been in operation here for decades. Savi was one of the elders of Black Spire Outpost, cornering the market on scrap metals years ago. While his main office and workshop is in town, much of the action takes place out here at the junkyard. They'll buy and trade just about any piece of old metal, but their primary focus is abandoned and broken-down ships. When an old vessel just isn't worth the hassle to fix, Savi and his crew will buy it for its scrap value. Unfortunately for the customer, the price that Savi offers is the only offer you're going to get out here.

The **scrappers**, as the locals call them, stick to what they know. Savi has earned a reputation among his workers for his kindness, calm nature, and wisdom. He doesn't let just anyone join their ranks. Those who do make it into his exclusive circle are treated well. They mostly keep to themselves and it's rare to see them about town. Their near obsession with old scrap means they have amassed quite the collection over the years. Their motto is fitting: "We'll take your (s)crap."

From the salvage yard, you can continue to travel farther in to the forest or head back toward town. The quiet dirt path that leads from the salvage yard to the market is known to the locals as **Savi's Path**. As I walk along this path, I often wonder, *Who was Savi's son*? In all my years traveling to Batuu, I've never seen old Savi's heir.

THE FOREST

THE FOREST

As you wander farther from the gates of Black Spire Outpost, you'll find yourself in Batuu's beautiful **forests**. A walk here reminds you of the planet's rich and mysterious past. Quiet, tree-lined paths lead to the last remains of an ancient civilization. All around you, the ancient petrified trees serve as a reminder of Batuu's ecological history.

ANCIENT RUINS

The ruins outside of Black Spire Outpost are one of Batuu's best-kept secrets. Some visitors might notice a set of stairs leading up the rock face, just one of many reminders that Batuu was once home to a long-lost civilization. The sound of a tranquil waterfall lures explorers deeper into the caverns where they will discover a peaceful pool. This space feels almost sacred, as if it served an important purpose for the beings who came before. From here, the most adventurous travelers can explore farther into the ruins. The walls and pillars inside show faded signs of the early inhabitants.

In recent days, the tranquility of the forest has given way to the hushed activity of off-worlders. In one nearby clearing, evidence of **Resistance** activity is mounting. Just far enough from the Outpost to avoid detection yet close enough to take advantage of the people and resources nearby, this area would make an ideal center of operations. Batuuans share reports of Resistance ships—both starfighters and larger transport ships alike—coming and going from the clearings and ruins not far from Black Spire. The increased traffic of astromech droids alone suggests that something is afoot. No matter what is going on out there, it's clear that those who venture into the clearing return with a renewed sense of hope and optimism rarely seen in the Outpost.

Exploring the Batuu wilderness was already risky enough before reports of the Resistance's arrival, so I urge all travelers to exercise caution when exploring outside the Outpost walls at this time. You might not want to find yourself caught in the middle of the ongoing political struggles.

THE PEOPLE: RESISTANCE MILITARY & LEADERS

Staunch believers in peace, freedom, and justice, members of the **Resistance** stand in stark contrast to the soldiers of the First Order. Whereas the stormtroopers are models of faceless uniformity, Resistance troops embrace their individuality. They lack the state-of-the-art arms and equipment of their adversaries, instead making do with Republic surplus. Every member is a volunteer, choosing to join the cause of the Resistance for reasons that are always idealistic and often deeply personal.

The most famous member of the Resistance is its founder, **General Leia Organa.** The former Rebel and senator founded the Resistance to fight back against the threat of the First Order. Back then, most didn't even know there was a First Order and almost everyone else didn't see them as a threat. Organa and her loyal followers armed themselves with aging military equipment and prepared for the coming fight. She and her Resistance fighters are being hunted by the First Order.

In recent days, the name **Vi Moradi** has gained notoriety around Black Spire Outpost. Moradi is said to be a member of the Resistance and a talented spy, and the First Order believes her to be connected to a rebel cell here on Batuu. It seems like everyone—Resistance sympathizer and First Order loyalist alike—is looking for Vi Moradi.

SHIPS OF THE RESISTANCE:
INTERSYSTEM TRANSPORT SHIP

Manufacturer: Corellian Engineering Corporation
Model: Intersystem Transport Ship (I-TS)
Class: Transport
Crew: 1 pilot, 1 copilot, 1 flight engineer (optional)
Armament: 2 twin medium laser cannons (forward)
Affiliation: Resistance

DRIVE TURBINE COOLING VANE

DEFLECTOR SHIELD GENERATOR

COCKPIT VIEWPORT

SUBLIGHT ION ENGINES

HYPERDRIVE

TWIN MEDIUM LASER CANNONS

LANDING GEAR ACTUATOR

TRANSPARISTEEL VIEWPORTS

SUBSPACE COMMUNICATIONS

CABIN ACCESS HATCH

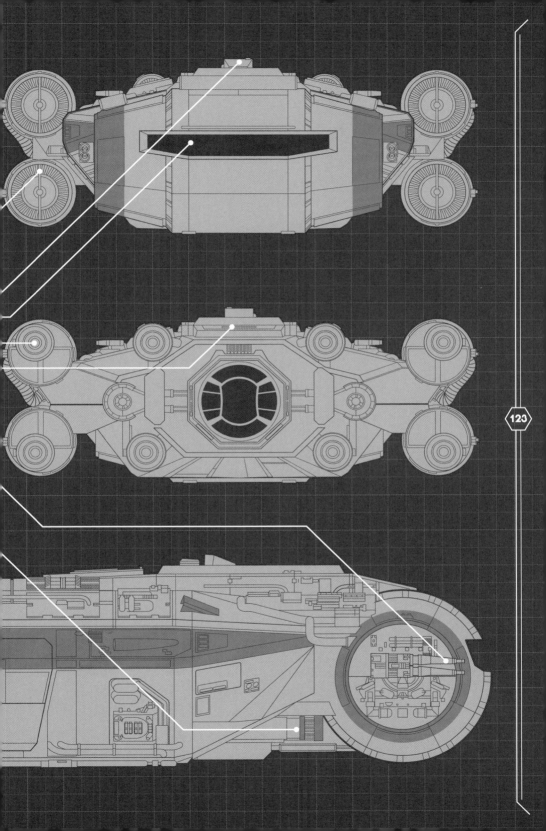

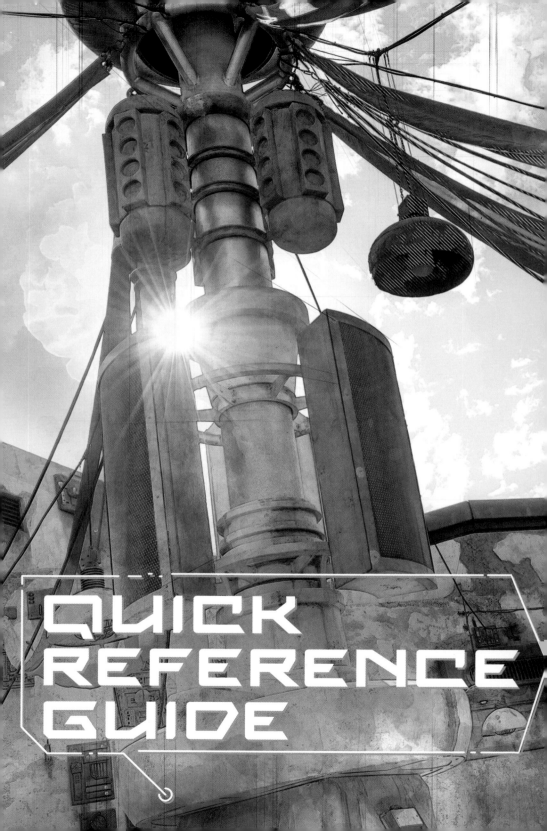

QUICK
REFERENCE
GUIDE

AUREBESH

A	B	C	D
E	F	G	H
I	J	K	L
M	N	O	P
Q	R	S	T
U	V	W	X
Y	Z		

SYMBOLS & EMBLEMS

As you walk the streets of the Black Spire Outpost, various icons, symbols, and emblems adorn banners, walls, and signs. Easy recognition of these symbols may make navigating the Outpost a bit easier and potentially help keep you from wandering someplace you don't want to be.

DROID DEPOT

OGA'S CANTINA

DOK-ONDAR'S DEN OF ANTIQUITIES

SAVI & SONS SALVAGE

OHNAKA TRANSPORT SOLUTIONS

DOCKING BAY 7

RONTO ROASTERS

KAT SAKA'S KETTLE

LOCAL HOLIDAYS

Batuu has a number of unique traditions including three major annual holidays.

BLACK SPIRE DAY

Black Spire Day, celebrated every May fourth, commemorates the founding of the Outpost. On this happy holiday locals decorate the Outpost with pieces like colorful tarps, ribbons, and flowers. Locals sing traditional songs, feast, and tie wishes to the Trilon tree. Sometimes the evening ends in a procession through the Outpost with a fireworks display.

BATUUAN HARVEST FESTIVAL

This autumnal event celebrates the bounty of the harvest season. In particular, Batuuans honor their most valuable natural resource, golden lichen, or "gold dust" as the locals call it. Only during this festival does crime boss Oga Garra consider allowing her valuable commodity of golden lichen to be used in special drinks and dishes. The Outpost itself is decorated in golden hued banners streamers, and locals have been known to enhance their garb with similar colors.

LIFE DAY

This longstanding Wookiee tradition has been embraced by beings across the galaxy. On Batuu, locals celebrate the ideals of peace, harmony, and freedom for all beings no matter how different they may appear. Festive decor can be seen throughout Batuu and at the close of Life Day everyone gathers around the black spire to sing songs and spread good cheer to one another.

HELPFUL PHRASES

Thanks to Batuu's remote position in the galaxy and its diverse mix of inhabitants that colonized the planet long ago, the residents have adopted some unique words and phrases over time. As you travel through the streets of Black Spire Outpost or meet with farmers in the far-flung communities, use these words to help you fit in with the locals.

"THE OUTPOST," "BSO"	BLACK SPIRE OUTPOST
"THE OLD POST"	THE ANCIENT RUINS AROUND BSO
"THE PORT"	SPACEPORT
"GOLD DUST"	GOLDEN LICHEN, GROWS ON BATUU
"BRIGHT SUNS"	HELLO (DAYTIME)
"RISING MOONS"	HELLO (NIGHTTIME)
"MAY YOUR DEALS GO WELL"	GOOD LUCK
"MAY THE SPIRES KEEP YOU"	FAREWELL
"'TIL THE SPIRE"	FAREWELL
"WELL BARTERED"	THANK YOU
"AND YOU"	YOU'RE WELCOME
"ONLY THE ANCIENTS KNOW"	I DON'T KNOW
"THANK THE SKIES!"	THANK GOODNESS

When taking your first drink in the cantina, it is customary to cheers to your mates by saying "Now and 'til the Spire," "Under the shadow of the Spire," or "Here's to a good run!"

PACKING LIST & LUGGAGE

TECHNOLOGY

- ☐ Comlink
- ☐ Datapad
- ☐ Imaging unit to take holoscans
- ☐ Holoprojector (optional, for long trips)

CARGO

- ☐ Comfortable boots or shoes
- ☐ Credits or credit chip
- ☐ Deck of sabacc cards or other games

FIELD GEAR

- ☐ Electrobinoculars or quadnoculars
- ☐ Utility belt with pouches
- ☐ Rebreather, if planning to dive underwater
- ☐ Grappling hook
- ☐ Walking staff
- ☐ Gloves
- ☐ Goggles
- ☐ Helmet

TRAVELERS WITH DROIDS

- ☐ Recharger
- ☐ Rocket booster fuel
- ☐ Droid caller

TRAVELERS WITH FUR

- ☐ Hairdryer
- ☐ Comb or brush

WHAT NOT TO PACK

Guide maps and chrono guides. These are available upon your arrival. Blasters (you'll find nothing but trouble) death sticks, spice, or other illegal substances: Invasive species, including reptiles, birds, and fish.

LUGGAGE

A simple rucksack is the most common piece of cargo carried by visitors to Batuu. With careful planning, a single pack should be enough for a standard day trip to the planet and even a long weekend. Longer journeys might require more substantial luggage, but please consider that transporting such heavy luggage can prove challenging throughout most of Batuu and will only draw unwanted attention in Black Spire Outpost.

AROUND THE GALAXY: LUGGAGE FIT FOR A QUEEN

Naboo royalty are renowned throughout the galaxy for their heavy packing. A single trip for the monarch required a full security detail, a team of butlers or handmaidens, and a carefully packed wardrobe for every possible occasion. Queen Soruna, who served nearly thirty years ago, was a notoriously light packer by royal standards, only requiring three outfits per day. One visit to the Royal Palace and you'll understand why luxury is expected by the monarchy.

SPECIES

Batuu plays home to an array of species from across the galaxy. These are but a few of the species you might encounter on your visit.

BLUTOPIAN

Homeworld: Blutopia

With grey skin and distinctive mouth tentacles, members of this species can't be missed. They are a strong, stout species that can hold their own in rough situations. The outpost's boss and cantina owner, Oga Garra, is a Blutopian.

RODIAN

Homeworld: Rodia

Green, red and orange-skinned Rodians are a common sight throughout the galaxy. Work or pleasure lures them to Batuu, though it is far less humid than their native planet, Rodia.

HUTT

Homeworld: Nal Hutta

Hutts are best known for their language,
Huttese, which is commonly spoken
throughout the galaxy. They are also
famous as gangsters and criminal leaders.
Hutts have a reputation wherever they go,
so if you encounter one during your travels it's
recommended you avoid upsetting them at all costs.

HUMAN

Homeworld: Various

Like so many other planets across the
galaxy, Humans are the most common
species you will encounter on Batuu.
Humans make up the largest population of
offworlders and locals alike.

PANTORAN

Homeworld: Pantora

These humanoids are easily spotted thanks
to their blue skin and golden eyes. They hail
from a moon in the Outer Rim.

ZABRAK

Homeworld: Iridonia

Members of the Zabrak species are most easily identified by the horns atop their heads. They are sometimes called Iridonians.

NIKTO

Homeworld: Kintan

Depending on where they come from on their home planet of Kintan, Nikto can have different skin tones and facial features. They are especially known for their toughness, so they often serve as guards and bounty hunters.

WEEQUAY

Homeworld: Sriluur

The thick-skinned Weequay hail from a harsh desert planet. Perhaps it's this difficult environment that makes so many of this species resilient, resourceful beings. The loudest, most boisterous Weequay on Batuu is Hondo Ohnaka.

ITHORIAN

Homeworld: Ithor

The local collector and shop owner Dok-Ondar is an Ithorian, sometimes referred to as a "hammerhead." Since their vocal cords can't produce the sounds to speak Basic, they often rely on translators (either droids or beings) to help them communicate. Ithorians are generally considered to be excellent gardeners.

UTAI

Homeworld: Utapau

Small and curious people, the Utai hail from the Outer Rim planet of Utapau. They share their homeworld with the Amani, and the much taller Pau'ans. Combining the names of these two species inspired the planet's name ("Uta" + "pau"). The local droid mechanic, Mubo, is a member of this species.

MIRIALAN

Homeworld: Mirial

Green, yellow or purple-skinned Mirialan are another humanoid species you might encounter. Tattoos on their faces are another way to tell them from other species.

GAMES ON BATUU

Across the planet and throughout Black Spire Outpost, Batuuans love playing sabacc. The popular card game brings together beings from all walks of life. It's a deceptively simple game where fortunes are won (and lost) thanks to skill and perhaps more than a bit of luck. For thrill seekers, few activities compare to playing high-stakes games. The less fortunate and downtrodden are just one hand away from potentially turning their luck around.

I myself have seen more than 80 forms of sabacc played across the galaxy. The most common variant on Batuu requires 62 cards and two six-sided chance cubes. Generally speaking, the game is played with a dealer and two to eight players, for three rounds, with the goal being to score as close to zero as possible. Between each round, the dealer rolls the chance cubes, and if they roll a double, all players' cards are placed in the discard pile. The dealer will then deal each player the same amount of cards they discarded. If the dice are different, each player keeps their cards. After all three rounds are played, the player with the best hand wins. "Pure Sabacc," zero with exactly two zero cars, is unbeatable.

Be wary of anyone who claims to be new at sabacc and asks you to play a few hands. Chances are they're looking to lure an unsuspecting off-worlder into a game. After a few hands and many lost credits, visitors realize they have been hustled by one of Black Spire's skilled card players.

SABACC
CARDS

HOLOCHESS

While no one remembers when the game known as dejarik (or simply as holochess) was likely brought to the planet by traveling pilots, it has taken hold with some of the more thoughtful and strategic residents of the Outpost. Players confident in their skills might consider competing in the Batuuan Holochess Tournament, an event popular enough to be broadcast on the local frequency.

CHANCE CUBES

Another game you might encounter on Batuu is the **chance cube**. Playing is as simple as rolling the cubes and seeing which side lands face up, but the real excitement lies is wagering credits on the outcome. Weighted cubes, made specifically for cheating, aren't common but occasionally turn up. Those found cheating are rarely seen or heard from again in the Outpost.

AROUND THE GALAXY: CASINOS

While Batuu mostly offers intimate card games played between a few travelers in a humble cantina, the casinos on Cantonica are home to world-class gaming in famously lavish surroundings. The casino city of Canto Bight is a must-see for the ultra rich.

ABOUT THE AUTHOR

Eloc Throno is a historian and author with twenty years' experience traveling the galaxy. After leaving his home planet of Davnar, he studied cartography at the Graf Archive on the moon Orchis 2 under director Amel Fortoon. He's the author of more than a dozen travel guides and makes frequent appearances on regional HoloNet programming. He believes the best way to learn about galactic history is to visit a place first hand, meet its people, and live like the locals do.

Other Books by Eloc Throno

The Traveler's Guide to Tatooine
From Shrikes Peak to the Dune Sea

The Traveler's Guide to Xibariz
A Journey Through Perpetual Twilight

Volcanic Planets: Your Guide to the Galaxy's Hottest Destinations
Mustafar, Sullust, Shu-Torun, and More

Mandalorian Battlefield Tours
*In Partnership with the
Sundari Historical Preservation Association*

LANDING PERMIT

VESSEL NAME:

ᐯᛕᐱᐱᐯᛕᐱ ᐊᛕᛕᐯᛖ:

MODEL:

ᛕᐅᒎᐯᛕ:

LANDING DATE:

ᐱᛕᐱᒎᛕᐅᛒ ᒎᛕᛕᐱᛖ:

TRANSMIT DOCKING CODES TO FREQUENCY

ᛕᒎᛕᛕᐱᛕᒎᛕ ᒎᐅᛕᒎᛒᐅᛒ ᛕᐅᒎᐱᛕ ᛕᐅ ᛕᒎᐱᛕᛕᐱᛕᒎ

$$\boxed{1104.517.0004}$$

PERMIT VALID FOR 1 2 3 4 5 6 7 DAYS:

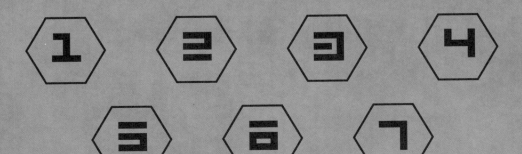

Disney · LUCASFILM

© & TM 2020 Lucasfilm.
www.starwars.com

Published in 2020 by becker&mayer! books, an imprint of The Quarto Group, 11120 NE 33rd Place, Suite 201, Bellevue, WA 98004 USA.
www.QuartoKnows.com

becker&mayer! books titles are also available at discount for retail, wholesale, promotional, and bulk purchase. For details, contact the Special Sales Manager by email at specialsales@quarto.com or by mail at The Quarto Group, Attn: Special Sales Manager, 100 Cummings Center Suite 265D, Beverly, MA 01915 USA.

18 19 20 21 22   5 4 3 2 1

ISBN: 978-0-7603-6674-5

Library of Congress Cataloging-in-Publication Data available upon request.

Lucasfilm:
Senior Editor: Brett Rector
Art Director: Troy Alders
Creative Director of Publishing: Michael Siglain
Story Group: James Waugh, Pablo Hidalgo, Leland Chee, Matt Martin
Image Asset Team: Tim Mapp, Gabrielle Levenson, Nicole LaCoursiere, Sarah Williams

Walt Disney Imagineering:
Creative Executive: Scott Trowbridge
Assistant Producer: Stacey Leong
Managing Story Editor: Margaret Kerrison
Asset Specialist: Carter Tata
Senior Producer: Raina Ross
Producer: Rachel Sherbill

Becker&Mayer!:
Author: Cole Horton
Design: Scott Richardson
Park Map Illustration: David White
Illustration: Chris Trevas and Chris Reiff
Editorial: Meredith Mennitt
Production: Tom Miller

Image credits: Kent Phillips, Matt Stroshane, David Roark, Don Saban, Mike Pucher, Chloe Rice, Gabrielle Biasi, David Nguyen, Allison Friedlander. Art credits: Christian Alzmann, Brett Northcutt

Printed, manufactured, and assembled in China, 03/20.

329797